Lovestories 4 Girls

Flirt But Don't Fall in Love

Julia Ross

Compact Verlag

Bisher sind in dieser Reihe erschienen:

Band 1: Full Moon Kisses
Band 2: Last Chance for a First Date
Band 3: Flirt But Don't Fall in Love
Band 4: Trouble in Seventh Heaven

Weitere Titel sind in Vorbereitung.

Chefredaktion: Dr. Angela Sendlinger
Redaktion: Paulina Palomino
Fachredaktion: Yasmin und Richard Robinson
Produktion: Wolfram Friedrich
Illustrationen: Bettina Weisl (MA Illustration)
Typografischer Entwurf: textum GmbH
Umschlaggestaltung: Bettina Weisl (MA Illustration)

ISBN: 978-3-8174-7824-8
7278241

Besuche uns im Internet: www.compactverlag.de

Vorwort

Mit dieser spannenden und romantischen Compact Lovestory kannst du deine Englischkenntnisse spielend leicht verbessern. Eine deutsche Einleitung vor jedem neuen Kapitel hilft dir, den englischen Text zu verstehen. Außerdem werden auf jeder Seite die etwas schwierigeren Wörter erklärt, und durch die Zeichnungen bekommst du eine genauere Vorstellung von den vier Girls und ihren aufregenden Erlebnissen. Blätter doch einfach mal durch!

Jedes Kapitel wird durch Übungen und Tests ergänzt, die richtig spannend und abwechslungsreich sind: Da geht es um Jungs und Liebe, Partys, Freundschaft und Mode – so wird Englisch lernen richtig spannend und cool!

Die Antworten und Lösungen kannst du gleich ins Buch schreiben und hinterher im Lösungsteil nachlesen, ob du alles richtig gemacht hast und was die Tests über dich aussagen. Und wenn du möchtest, kannst du alle Vokabeln im Glossar noch einmal nachschlagen. Slang-Ausdrücke sind mit einem ϟ gekennzeichnet.

Wir wünschen dir viel Spaß mit Holly und ihren Freundinnen – und natürlich viel Erfolg beim Englisch lernen!

Inhalt

1

A Dream Comes True

1

Holly träumt lieber von Jungs und Musikbands anstatt dem Schulunterricht zu folgen. Als sie auf einer Party Matt kennen lernt, der in einer Band spielt, ist sie total begeistert. Und als er ihr Gitarrenunterricht anbietet, ist sie vollkommen hin und weg – ihr Traum scheint zum Greifen nah! Der Talentwettbewerb ihrer Schule liefert ihr den perfekten Vorwand, täglich Unterricht bei Matt zu nehmen …

"Holly Brown! I've asked you three times now!"
The loud, angry voice woke up Holly from her daydream. When she looked up, she saw her geography teacher, Miss Hamilton, staring straight at her. She was impatiently pointing at a map of Africa.
"So, for the fourth time, would you please tell the class the name of the famous river that I am pointing at? Or is whatever is happening outside that window more interesting?"
Holly's cheeks turned pink as she thought about the question. The truth was that she had not simply been looking out of the window. Instead she had been lost in a daydream about meeting her favourite boy band. And it had certainly not had anything to do with the geography of Africa.

Her friend Emily nudged her gently, whispering a short word that Holly did not hear.
"Uh...," she began.
Miss Hamilton was still looking at her angrily, with her glasses perched on the end of her large nose.
Under the table, Emily was still trying to get Holly's attention. She pointed down at a page of extremely organized notes and circled a word.
"The answer is... the... the River Nile!" said Holly, as she read the word from the page Emily had given to her.
She looked very relieved. So did Emily, who finally stopped nudging Holly's leg.
Holly looked down at her own notes and noticed that they were crumpled and covered with little drawings of flowers and hearts. She tried to look like she was thinking hard, and carefully wrote the word 'Nile' underneath one of the drawings.
When the bell rang a minute later, Holly rushed to leave so quickly that she almost fell over her own chair. When she met her friends Emily, Evie and Nina outside the classroom, she thanked Emily for helping her.
"Thank you so much for saving me in there!" she said. "My mind was completely blank. I'm terrible at geography. Well,

impatiently	ungeduldig
cheek	Wange
to nudge	(an)stupsen
gently	sanft, behutsam
to perch on sth.	auf etw. sitzen
attention	Aufmerksamkeit
relieved	erleichtert
crumpled	zerknüllt
to rush	eilen, rennen
blank	leer

ÜBUNG 1: True or false? Kreuze die richtigen Aussagen an.

1. Holly tries hard at school, but Emily distracts her by passing notes to her under the table. ☐
2. Holly finds school difficult because of her bad memory. She often forgets things. ☐
3. Miss Hamilton gets angry at Holly because she has not listened to what the teacher has said. ☐
4. Holly makes Miss Hamilton angry by talking to Emily in class. ☐
5. The teacher gets angry at Holly because instead of making notes she draws hearts and flowers. ☐

geography and history... and English, maths and science..."
"No you aren't, you just never concentrate. You'd probably be top of the class if you ever listened to the teachers!" said Evie, laughing.
"No way, not with Emily in all my classes!" Holly replied. "And no-one could ever beat you in PE, Evie."
"If there was a subject about boy bands, Holly would get 100% in every test," joked Nina.

"Yeah, especially if there were bonus questions about Mr Stubbs!" added Evie.
The girls all knew about Holly's crush on their English teacher. Holly blushed at the mention of his name, which made the others giggle even more.

No way!	Nie im Leben!
to beat sb.	jmd. schlagen (besiegen)
PE (physical education)	Sport(unterricht)
subject	*hier:* Unterrichtsfach
crush	Schwärmerei

"I told you, I don't like him like that anymore. Really, I don't!"
"It doesn't matter anyway," said Nina, "maybe you'll meet someone new to daydream about at that party tonight..."
Emily nodded. "Yeah, that's true. I heard that loads of boys from the year above are coming. Hey, look, Holly, Matt's over there, why don't you go and ask him if he'll be at the party?"
Holly was horrified at the idea.
"No way, he's so good-looking – I'd probably forget how to speak if I ever got near him!"
They all laughed. "Well, we should go," Holly continued. "I want to choose my outfit for tonight!" They picked up their things and started to walk home, talking about what each of them would wear at the party.

to blush	erröten, rot werden
mention	Erwähnung
to giggle	kichern
to nod	nicken
loads of	eine Menge
horrified	entsetzt

ÜBUNG 2: What's your fashion style? Kreuze an.

1. How do you get ready in the morning?
   a) ❑ I spend about half an hour choosing the right outfit. I won't leave the house unless I look perfect.
   b) ❑ I choose my outfit the night before, so that I don't have to think about it in the morning.
   c) ❑ I usually sleep too late so I generally choose the first things that I can find on my floor.

2. Which of these outfits would you prefer to wear?
   a) ❑ A top and knee-length skirt with matching bag and shoes, and lots of jewellery.
   b) ❑ Something practical that is suitable for all the things that I want to do that day, but still looks nice.
   c) ❑ A comfortable jumper and jeans, with trainers.

3. Which of these situations do you think is the worst?
   a) ❑ A boy that you like sees you with greasy hair.
   b) ❑ You can't take part in outdoor activities because you are wearing a skirt and sandals.
   c) ❑ You're going to a wedding, so you have to spend a lot of time getting ready.

4. Which of these people would you most admire?
   a) ❑ A glamorous film star.
   b) ❑ An Olympic athlete.
   c) ❑ A rock star.

advice	Rat
slightly	leicht, ein bisschen
chubby	mollig
waist	Taille

Later that evening, Holly changed her outfit five times and called each of her three best friends for advice in order to get ready for the party. In the end, she chose a black dress with a beautiful silver belt that hid her slightly chubby waist. She and Nina had decided to walk to the party together, so Holly called at Nina's house once she was finally ready. A few minutes later the two of them left, a little later than they had planned.

flattering	schmeichel-haft
to be about to do sth.	im Begriff sein, etw. zu tun
to burst	(zer)platzen
excitement	Aufregung
to guess	erraten, vermuten
overhear	belauschen
reassurance	Bestätigung

When they arrived at the party, Emily and Evie met them at the door, each in a flattering top and skirt. Emily looked as though she were about to burst with excitement. Her expression made Holly think of their geography class earlier that day, when Emily had tried to let her know the answer in class without saying it out loud. This time Emily even put her hand over her own mouth as if to stop the information from escaping. She quickly took Holly by the hand and went into the garden with her.

"Holly you'll never guess what! It's Matt, he's right there." Emily was whispering now and pointing to the doorway. "I overheard him talking to Nathan a minute ago, and he said he really likes you!"

"What?! I didn't think he even knew my name!"

"I know! Well, actually, he didn't say your name *exactly*... but the way he described the girl he liked, it had to be you. He was describing some-one that looks just like you, who wears that hair band with the hearts on that you often put in your hair. It must be you!"

"Do you think I should go and talk to him?" Holly asked nervously, looking to her friend for reassurance.

ÜBUNG 3: Fill in the blanks. Vervollständige die Sätze mit den angegebenen Wörtern!

crush *chubby* *flattering* *blushed*

horrified *burst* *overheard*

1. Holly wore a beautiful silver belt that hid her slightly .... waist.
2. Both Emily and Evie wore a .... top and skirt.
3. The girls all knew about Holly's .... on their English teacher.
4. Emily .... Matt talking to Nathan.
5. Emily looked as though she were about to .... with excitement.
6. Holly .... when Evie mentioned Mr Stubbs.
7. She was .... at the idea of speaking to Matt.

"Of course! Just relax. He already likes you, and you look beautiful tonight. Don't worry!"

Although Emily's words had given Holly more confidence, she still felt shy. Over an hour had passed since their conversation, but she was still talking to the girls and trying to find the courage to speak to Matt. She wished that she could be like Evie, who was confidently discussing sport with a group of older boys. An hour had already become two before she realized that if she waited much longer she would miss her chance completely.

She saw that there was an empty seat next to Matt, so she sat next to him and shyly said hello. She was glad that so far she had managed not to say anything embarrassing.

"Hi, how's it going?" responded Matt.

His smile made her knees feel like jelly. Holly felt her mind going blank again.

"Uh... great, thanks."

"Yeah, it's a cool party, isn't it? The music's been good. Do you like this band?"

Holly smiled at her good luck: the song that was playing was by one of her favourite boy bands and she knew every word of it.

"I love them!" she replied. "I prefer 'Never Say Never' out of the songs on this album, but this one is brilliant, too."

courage	Mut
confidently	selbstbewusst
glad	froh
embarrassing	peinlich
jelly	Wackelpudding
to prefer	lieber mögen, vorziehen

Matt agreed, and then added, "It's really easy to play, too."
"Wow, it sounds quite difficult to me!" said Holly. "Which instrument do you play?"
"The guitar," he replied. "I've only been learning for about a year, but I'm in a band, so I play stuff like this all the time."
Holly's heart skipped a beat. In her head she pictured the band she'd been dreaming about earlier but replaced the lead singer's face with Matt's. She wondered whether this could be the perfect chance for her dream love to finally come true.

to add	hinzufügen
to skip a beat	einen Schlag aussetzen (Herz)
to picture sth.	sich etw. vorstellen
to remind	erinnern
complicated	kompliziert
suggestion	Vorschlag

A moment later, reminding herself that this was real life and not one of her daydreams, Holly remembered that it was her turn to say something.
"Being in a band really sounds fun. I started learning how to play the guitar last summer, but I'm sure I couldn't play anything as complicated as this."
"It's really not that difficult," said Matt. "Maybe I could show you one day?"
Holly had to stop herself from letting him see just how happy his suggestion had made her.
With difficulty she managed to stay calm and said, "That would be cool. I'll give you my number, and we can meet up some time soon."

After she had given Matt her phone number, Holly returned to find her best friends and tell them all about what had just happened. Emily was in the garden with Matt's friend Nathan, and the two of them seemed to be having a lot of fun together. Holly did not want to interrupt. Luckily she saw the other two on the stairs and ran to tell them the news.

"That's fantastic!" cried Nina, and stood up to give her friend a hug. "You two would make such a good couple!"

"Don't be silly! I only have his number; it doesn't mean we're going to be a couple."

"I bet you'll be daydreaming about it all day at school tomorrow though!" said Evie, teasing Holly affectionately. "By the way," she added, "I've arranged to play football with some of his friends tomorrow. Maybe he'll be there, too."

"Hmm, perhaps I'll come along, too, then," said Holly and smiled. "Just to watch you of course..."

ÜBUNG 4: Grammatically correct? Kreuze an.

1. Holly speaked to Matt about music, and he told her that he played the guitar in a band. ❑
2. Holly to Matt spoke about music, and he telled her that he played the guitar in a band. ❑
3. Holly spoke to Matt about music, and he told her that he played the guitar in a band. ❑

The next day, Holly persuaded Nina and Emily to go to the sports centre with her to watch Evie play football. This way it would not look like she had just come to see Matt. But when they got there, the game had already started, and he was not there. Nathan had just arrived, too, so Emily went to talk to him. Meanwhile, Nina chatted to a boy she knew from the German Club. She had started the club at school to teach her native language to the other students.

Holly sat by the side of the football pitch on her own and was soon daydreaming again. She imagined Matt playing a love song to her on his guitar. Then she noticed that her neighbour Daniel had scored a goal. Holly thought she saw him wave to her but did not wave back. Although they had been childhood friends, she had not spoken to him for a while and thought he must be waving to someone else.

Then her mobile phone made a sound, so she took it out of her pocket to see who had sent her a text.

She gasped when she read the sender's name: Matt.

to interrupt	unter-brechen
hug	Umarmung
couple	Paar
though	aber, doch
to tease	necken, ärgern
affectionately	liebevoll
to persuade	überreden
to chat	plaudern
pitch	Feld
to imagine sth.	sich etw. vorstellen
to score a goal	ein Tor schießen
to wave	winken
text (message)	SMS
to gasp	nach Luft ringen

The text message read:

Hey Holly, how about a guitar lesson tomorrow? Matt x

Later that evening, Holly was using the computer in her bedroom when her mobile rang. She had already replied to Matt's text, but now that he was calling her she immediately felt very nervous. Without thinking she hid the phone under her pillow and tried to ignore it. Her pillow continued to ring loudly. She eventually decided that she should answer.

to hide	verstecken
pillow	Kopfkissen
eventually	schließlich
casual	lässig, locker
to promise	versprechen
barely	kaum
cheerful	aufgekratzt

"Oh, hi, Matt," she said, trying to sound casual. "I hope I haven't kept you waiting long. I was listening to the radio and didn't hear the phone."

"No problem," Matt said. "I was just calling about that guitar lesson. Are you free tomorrow after school?"

"Yeah!" replied Holly rather loudly. She tried to sound calmer when she added, "I mean I think I'll be free for an hour or two."

"Great," said Matt. "Meet me outside school and we can go back to my house. See you tomorrow then."

"See you! Bye!" Holly said, jumping onto her bed as she hung up the phone. She was so excited and happy that she gave her teddy bear a big kiss.

The next day after school, Matt walked with Holly to his house. As he had promised, he showed her how to play the song, but they talked for so long that they barely managed to play the guitar for ten minutes. Back at home that evening, Holly was even more cheerful than she had been the night before. And even though posters of boy bands covered all of the walls of her bedroom, she did not think of any of them for a minute. Instead, all of her daydreams were filled with thoughts of Matt.

ÜBUNG 5: *Fill in the blanks! Setze die richtige Variante ein.*

1. Holly was .... when Matt .... her to his house.

   a) delighted, invited
   b) distraught, introduced
   c) devoted, inserted

2. Holly does not really .... watching football ....

   a) interest, pitches
   b) enjoy, matches
   c) notice, goals

3. Holly .... a text message from Matt while she is sitting at the .... of the pitch.

   a) results, side
   b) sends, corner
   c) receives, edge

to spot	erblicken
notice board	Schwarzes Brett
prize	Gewinn
mark	Schulnote
to suppose	annehmen, denken
contest	Wettbewerb
in unison	einstimmig
to sign up	sich anmelden

Later that week, Holly, Evie, Nina and Emily were meeting up after school to walk home together as usual. Then Evie spotted a poster on the notice board. "Have you seen this?" she asked them. "Look, there's going to be a talent show at the school, and the prize is a hundred pounds! Think of all the clothes we could buy with that!" She thought for a minute, before adding, "It's a shame I can't play football on the stage as my talent."

"Don't worry, I can't exactly do maths or get a good mark in an exam on stage for mine!" said Emily. "I suppose none of our talents make for a very good show."

They were about to forget about the whole idea when Holly had a thought: if she entered the contest, perhaps she could ask Matt to help her practise.

"I'm still learning the guitar," she said. "I could enter."

"Yeah!" said the other girls in unison. Nina told her, "You should definitely enter. Imagine winning that prize!"

"I don't think I'll win, but..."

Emily interrupted her. "If you practise really hard, you might do."

It was exactly what Holly wanted to hear. She couldn't imagine anything better than hours of guitar practice with Matt.

"I'll sign up right now!" she said.

distracted	abgelenkt
to improve	verbessern
to wince	zusammen-zucken
strings	Saiten
to sweat	schwitzen
to enter a competition	sich für einen Wettbewerb anmelden
to admit	zugeben
playfully	scherzhaft

Over the next two weeks, Holly did meet up with Matt for guitar practice several times. Each time, however, she would be easily distracted by their conversations and never seemed to improve her playing much. Matt remembered that Holly loved the song "Never Say Never", so he had suggested that she should learn it for the contest. But so far he had not even taught her the first part of the song.

As he listened to her play yet another wrong note, wincing at the ugly sound, he put his hand across the strings and said,

"Are you really sure you want to play this in the contest? I don't mean to upset you at all, but Hol, you're making my ears hurt!"

Holly laughed. "It's not as bad as your singing," she joked.

"Seriously though," Matt said. "I'm starting to wonder... wonder whether..."

"Whether what?" asked Holly nervously.

"Whether you're learning the guitar for the right reasons," he finally replied.

Holly suddenly felt herself begin to sweat. She was worried that he knew why she had entered the competition, and that he would not want to see her anymore.

Holly blushed and admitted, "I just wanted to spend time with you, I guess. I'm really sorry. I've wasted your time."
Matt looked surprised, but hit her on the arm playfully.

ÜBUNG 6: How does Holly feel? Enträtsele die Definition und finde die Lösung!

1. A school subject to do with numbers ... ▮ T ... S
2. Some of your favorite people ... R ... ... ▮ D ...
3. You can put things into it to keep them safe B ... ▮
4. A sport that is done in water ... W ... ... M ▮ N ...
5. You use this to tell the time ... L ▮ C ...
6. You arrive somewhere after a J ... ▮ ... ... E Y
7. Something that you can't tell anyone ▮ E ... R ... ...

Lösung: ... ...

painful	schmerzhaft
to flip	einen Salto schlagen
to offer	anbieten
to lean forward	sich vorbeugen
clumsy	unbeholfen
to take over	die Führung übernehmen

"Don't you worry, Holly Dolly. There's no reason to say sorry. Do you think I would have taught you guitar four times this week if I didn't like you, too? I just think maybe we should do something else together... something less painful for my ears."

She giggled. "Well, I *am* sorry about that!" she said.

"How about a date tonight instead?" he asked, and her heart flipped at the words. "I think Nathan and Emily are going to the cinema tonight, maybe we could go with them. What do you think?"

"I think that would be perfect," Holly replied.

The evening passed much too quickly. When they left the cinema Holly realized that she could not remember what had happened in the film, because she had been so distracted by Matt's hand touching hers. She did remember though that she had had the most wonderful night. Matt had made her laugh and held her hand, and one of her best friends had been there with her, too. She had really enjoyed trying to find moments when the two girls could whisper their secret excitement to each other.

But when they arrived at Emily's house, Nathan left, and it was just her and Matt, who had offered to walk home with her. When they arrived near her house, beneath one of the

street lights, he lent forward and kissed her on the lips. It was her first real kiss.
Holly had never felt anything like it before – she was excited and shy at the same time. She felt clumsy, but Matt seemed so confident that she stopped thinking and let her feelings take over.

After the kiss, neither of them knew what to say. They looked each other deeply in the eyes. "I have to go," Holly said at last. Matt nodded.

to collapse onto one's bed	aufs Bett fallen

"Good night, Hol. See you tomorrow."

Waving goodbye to Matt, she opened the door and went inside. Before her mother had even had time to ask her how her day had been, she had already run past her. She ran straight up to her room, where she once again collapsed happily onto her bed. Holly truly could not believe that this time she was not daydreaming.

2

Trouble in Paradise

2

Holly schwebt auf Wolke sieben. Sie ist total verliebt in Matt. Doch eines Tages erzählt er ihr, dass sie sich nach Ende des Trimesters nicht mehr sehen werden – Matt und seine Familie ziehen nach Schottland! Holly ist am Boden zerstört. Um über Matt hinwegzukommen trifft Holly sich mit ihren Freundinnen. An diesem Abend treffen Evie, Holly, Nina und Emily eine Abmachung: In Zukunft werden sie nur noch flirten und sich nie wieder verlieben!

Over the next few weeks, Holly was happy to find that she no longer needed excuses to see Matt. After she had admitted how she felt, they started to spend more time at each other's houses, but now they hardly ever played the guitar together. One thing that did not change, however, was the fact that Holly's mind was always filled with romantic thoughts about him. In fact, one day after school, she was so lost in her own imaginary world, that she began to stop listening to what the *real* Matt was saying to her.

"Holly? Are you listening?" asked Matt.

"Uh... yeah, of course," she replied. "That's...um... really cool."

"Cool? I'm surprised that you think that," said Matt, looking a little hurt.
Holly thought hard: she really could not remember what he had said to her just a minute ago. She hoped that she had not said the wrong thing.
Matt continued, "I don't think I'll be able to come and visit you very often at all. I'll be living so far away and I won't have much money for train tickets."

excuse	Ausrede
hardly ever	fast nie
imaginary	Schein-, Fantasie-
hurt	gekränkt
confused	verwirrt
to cut the ground from under sb.'s feet	jmd. den Boden unter den Füßen wegziehen
term	Trimester

"Wait, how far away? What?" asked Holly, who suddenly felt worried and confused.
"Don't you know that Glasgow is hundreds of miles away, Hol? It's a big city in Scotland. I guess you were serious when you told me that you're no good at geography!"
Holly felt like the ground had just been cut from under her feet. This time she had heard everything that Matt had said, but could not laugh at his joke. Instead she was simply trying to understand what was happening. Could Matt really be moving away to Scotland?
"Anyway," he added, "I don't think we're going to come back. My Dad has a new job there, and my parents have already sold our house. We're leaving at the end of term."
"But that's only two weeks away!"

"I know. Obviously they told me about it before, but I didn't want to mention it to you until it was definite. I didn't want to upset you for nothing."

obviously	natürlich, offensichtlich
to mention	erwähnen
definite	sicher, fest
to upset	beunruhigen
to punch	schlagen (mit der Faust)
to mumble	murmeln
to trickle down	herunterlaufen

Holly felt as though someone had punched her in the stomach. She did not want to cry, but she could feel the tears beginning to come. She knew that if she did not stop herself, they would soon be rolling down her hot cheeks.

"I think I should go," she said. "I need to think about this."

Matt did not stop her, but as she turned to leave, he touched her arm. "Look, you know I'm going to miss you. But we aren't going to be able to keep seeing each other once I've gone. It's just too far."

Holly could only manage to mumble a quiet "Okay." Then she quickly turned away, and the tears that had been waiting to fall started to trickle down her face.

ÜBUNG 7: Unscramble the text! Bringe die Ereignisse aus dem Text in die richtige Reihenfolge.

a) Holly is lost in a daydream and does not realize that Matt has just told her something very important.

b) Holly begins to cry.

c) Matt explains the reasons why his family are moving to Scotland.

d) Holly and Matt start to spend a lot of time together, although they don't play the guitar much anymore.

e) Matt tells Holly that Glasgow is much too far away from their home town for him to come and visit her.

f) Matt explains what type of place Glasgow is, and where it is located.

1	2	3	4	5	6	7

For the next two weeks, Holly tried to pretend that Matt was not really leaving, but the day that she had been dreading arrived too quickly. Again she had to hide her tears as she said goodbye to Matt before he and his family began their journey to Scotland and their new life far away from her.

Luckily she had her friends to comfort her. One weekend shortly after Matt had left for Glasgow, the four best friends decided to have a sleepover at Nina's house. Each of the girls brought their favourite film as well as a dessert. Holly began her second enormous bowl of ice cream as they watched Emily's choice of film, which was a love story with a sad ending. The film reminded Holly of how her own love story had ended so quickly.
She asked the others, "Do you think I should just forget about Matt? I felt like everything was going really well, but then it all ended so soon."
"It's sad," said Evie, "but maybe it would be best if you tried not to think about it so much."
Evie always tended to be quite practical about love and wanted to give her friend some helpful advice that would make her feel better.

to pretend	so tun, als ob
to dread sth.	etw. fürchten
to comfort sb.	jmd. trösten
sleepover	Übernachtung (bei Freunden)
bowl	Schüssel
to tend to	neigen zu

Nina seemed to strongly disagree. "But I think that you two were really good together," she said firmly. "If there's a chance that you could still see each other, then it's worth trying to stay in touch, however far away he lives."

firmly	nachdrücklich
to stay in touch	in Kontakt bleiben

"That's the problem – I have tried to stay in touch. I've written him e-mails, but he never replies."
Holly was already close to finishing her mountain of chocolate ice cream. Nina thought for a moment.
"Maybe Evie is right then. You don't want to get hurt even more."
Emily had been unusually quiet all evening, and now the other girls started to wonder why she had barely spoken. Holly looked over to her and saw that she, too, was looking a little upset, with her long dark hair covering most of her face.
"Em, are you alright? I know it's a sad film, but we've only watched about half an hour of it so far," she said.
"I'm fine," replied Emily. "It's nothing, really."
Evie put her arm around Emily and asked her what was wrong.
Eventually Emily admitted, "It's silly really. I shouldn't be so upset about it. It's just that I've been on a lot of dates with Nathan now, and I really thought he liked me. But when I asked him if he wanted to go to the school disco with me he said no. He must be taking someone else."

ÜBUNG 8: Reading comprehension.
Beantworte die Fragen zum Text!

1. What did the four girls bring to their sleepover, and where was it?

   ....

2. What makes Holly think about Matt at the sleepover?

   ....

3. Do Evie and Nina agree about whether Holly should try to forget about Matt?

   ....

4. Why is it difficult for Holly to stay friends with Matt?

   ....

5. What makes the other girls guess that Emily might be upset?

   ....

6. What did Holly eat at the sleepover?

   ....

"Oh no," said Holly, "there must be a reason. You and Nathan get along so well. I'm sure he wouldn't have asked another girl to go to the dance with him."

it's a shame	es ist eine Schande
to give sb. a makeover	jmd. stylen
enthusiastic	begeistert
to grab	(er)greifen
to suit sb.	jmd. stehen
before long	bald

Emily nodded sadly. "I thought that, too, but why else would he say no?"

"It's a shame, but there's no reason to get upset about it. Nathan and Matt must both be stupid, if they can't see how great you both are," said Nina.

Evie agreed. "Don't let them upset you. What we should do now is just to have some fun together and forget about boys for the night."

"That's right," said Holly. She did not want to spend a moment more thinking about Matt and how much he had upset her. "Let's all give each other makeovers! That will stop us from thinking about them for a while."

The other three girls were very enthusiastic about Holly's suggestion. Emily, who had been almost silent until then, suddenly grabbed her make-up bag and started to tell each of them which colours would suit them best. Nina suggested that they try on each other's clothes.

Before long they were all having a great time experimenting with brightly-coloured lipsticks and trying out different hairstyles.

curls	Locken
to flow	*hier:* wallen
to deserve	verdienen
wise	klug, weise

"We look brilliant!" said Nina excitedly as she looked at her new style in the mirror.
"Yeah, I love your hair like that," Emily replied and admired the golden curls that were flowing down Nina's shoulders.
"Thanks," Nina replied. "Your make-up really suits your green eyes, too."
Holly looked around at her friends, and she saw that every one of them looked beautiful and confident.
"We don't need boys to make us feel good," she said. "We have each other, and that's better than any boyfriend."
Her words made the other girls smile.
"Maybe we should be more careful about getting into relationships with boys anyway," added Emily. "We don't want them to lie to us or make us feel unhappy – none of us deserve to be treated that way."
"Yeah," said Holly, "we should never let that happen. We can flirt with them, but we shouldn't get too close."
"Flirt, but don't fall in love!" said Evie in agreement.
The others looked at Evie with the type of expression that suggested that she had just said something extremely wise and clever. They all said together: "Flirt, but don't fall in love!"
"That should be our motto from now on!" said Holly.

ÜBUNG 9: Verb forms. Setze die Verben in Klammern in die richtige Zeitform!

1. Holly *(think)* .... that all of her friends looked beautiful after their makeovers.
2. Their sleepover helped them to *(forget)* .... about the things that were upsetting them.
3. Holly *(decide)* .... that "Flirt, but don't fall in love" should be their motto.
4. Holly and Emily were both feeling sad before they *(go)* .... to the sleepover.

"Definitely," responded Emily. "We should all agree right now not to fall in love with anyone. Friends come before boyfriends, right?"
"Right!" said the others. They all shook hands to make their promise official and felt closer to each other than ever before.
The girls continued trying on clothes and make-up, laughing at silly jokes and telling each other secrets until it was

very late, and they were all beginning to feel sleepy. They were watching the third film of the evening when Holly asked the others which of the actors they liked best. She was surprised when no-one answered her, because she had not noticed how quickly the time had gone. Suddenly she heard a snoring sound coming from one of the sofas.

Realizing that she was the last one of the group awake, she tried to relax and go to sleep, but her thoughts kept her awake. Eventually, as she opened her eyes after trying to sleep for some time, she saw that outside it was beginning to get light.

Holly sat up and watched the sun rise over Nina's garden, bringing its soft colour to all the flowers and plants. She thought about what the other girls had said that night, and felt lucky to have such good friends.

snoring	schnarchend
to feel homesick	Heimweh haben

"What are you looking at?" asked Nina behind her.

Holly was surprised by the question, as she had thought that everyone was asleep.

"Oh, I was just thinking," she replied.

"I've been thinking a lot tonight as well," said Nina. "Since I moved to England I've made some brilliant friends, and I've realized that now I don't feel homesick for Germany anymore. I'm really happy!"

Holly smiled. "I'm really pleased for you," she said. "It must be difficult to leave your country and live somewhere that you don't know."
"As long as you have friends, you can feel at home anywhere," replied Nina.
She and Holly silently watched the sun come up before they finally fell asleep with the early morning light shining through the curtains.

ÜBUNG 10: Odd one out! Welches Wort ist das „schwarze Schaf"?

1. ice cream, marshmallows, cake, mashed potatoes
2. actress, film, quiz show, director
3. sunrise, evening, afternoon, morning
4. daisy, grass, rose, sunflower
5. friend, mate, companion, rival
6. pencil, rubber, dog, ink

to be pleased	sich freuen
curtain	Vorhang
whereas	wohingegen
miserable	unglücklich
absorbed	vertieft

A few days later at school, Holly noticed Emily chatting to an older boy, Adam, while Nathan spoke to a friend nearby. Emily looked very happy, and was laughing loudly and often, whereas Nathan seemed miserable. He kept looking over at Emily and her new friend, but Emily seemed too absorbed in the conversation to even notice that he was there.

Later on, Holly saw Nina and a tall, curly-haired boy talking together on the field. Nina looked very beautiful with her hair shining in the sun and a pretty silver necklace around her neck. Soon after, Nina found Holly at a bench nearby, and Nina told her about the conversation she had just had.

"Have you met Kieran before? I was just talking to him, and I really couldn't stop laughing. I hadn't really spoken to him much before now, but he's so funny."

"He's in my Spanish class, and he's always making jokes," replied Holly. "The other day he whispered a joke about the teacher to me, but she heard him and demanded to know what he had said. I thought she was going to be really angry, but in the end she found the joke so hilarious that she laughed as much as the rest of the class."

necklace	Halskette
to demand	verlangen
hilarious	urkomisch

ÜBUNG 11: Flirting style. Kreuze an, was auf dich zutrifft!

1. How nervous would you feel if you were talking to a boy that you fancy?
   a) ❑ I'm shy around boys and usually stay quiet if a boy that I like is nearby. *(2 points)*
   b) ❑ I wouldn't be nervous at all – I *love* talking to boys, especially when they are good-looking! *(5 points)*
   c) ❑ I don't feel shy talking to boys, but I don't find them very interesting. *(0 points)*

2. Which of these options do you think is your best feature?
   a) ❑ My looks. *(6 points)*
   b) ❑ My intelligence. *(2 points)*
   c) ❑ My kind and caring personality. *(4 points)*

3. Which of these things is most important?
   a) ❑ Hobbies and interests. *(0 points)*
   b) ❑ Family and friends. *(2 points)*
   c) ❑ Boys, definitely! *(5 points)*

4. Which of these options best describes you at a party?
   a) ☐ Sitting on the sofa, feeling shy. *(4 points)*
   b) ☐ Talking to lots of good-looking boys, and wearing a short skirt and tight top. *(6 points)*
   c) ☐ Outside in the garden talking to my best friend. *(2 points)*

While they talked, they noticed that Evie was sat with the captain of the football team. She had tied up her short red hair in the same style that they had showed her at the makeover.

"Everyone seems to be taking our promise seriously," said Holly. "The first part of the promise, at least..."

Nina laughed. "Well, *I* wasn't flirting anyway. I was just having a friendly conversation with Kieran!"

tied up	zusammengebunden
gorgeous	umwerfend

"And I'm sure Evie's having a very friendly conversation with Steve the gorgeous football player as well!" Holly joked.

Before long, the night of the school disco arrived. The girls had all decided that instead of agreeing to be anyone's date they would all just go together. They had also arranged to meet each other at Emily's house before it began so that they could help each other choose what to wear.

"Wow, you look incredible!" said Emily, as Holly came out of the bathroom wearing a knee-length red dress.

"Thanks," replied Holly with a smile. "You look great, too! I just hope that Nathan is there to see you... and realize how stupid he was not to come with you to the disco."

"I don't even care about that anymore to be honest," said Emily. "I'd rather be here with the three of you."

"I think we can all agree on that," said Evie.

When they arrived at the disco, wearing their carefully chosen outfits and subtle make-up, everyone seemed impressed. Adam, Kieran and Steve all complimented their appearance, and asked Emily, Nina and Evie to dance.

Holly began to find that her friends were so busy dancing and talking to the boys that she had to find other people to chat with. Soon she noticed Daniel, her neighbour, sitting by the side of the dance floor with his date Alicia. They were not dancing, as Alicia used a wheelchair. Holly went to speak to them both.

to arrange	verabreden, ausmachen
incredible	unglaublich
knee-length	knielang
honest	ehrlich
subtle	dezent
impressed	beeindruckt
to compliment sth.	über etw. Komplimente machen
wheelchair	Rollstuhl
properly	richtig

"Holly! I don't think I've properly spoken to you since we used to climb trees together in my garden!" said Daniel. "I thought I saw you at football a while ago, but it must not have been you."

"Er, no, I guess not," said Holly, although she remembered him waving to her at the football match.

"Have you met Alicia?" Daniel asked.

Alicia answered his question. "We know each other really well. We have loads of classes together."

"Yeah," added Holly. "Alicia is one of the people who have to wake me up when I fall asleep in class."

ϟ geek	Streber
to struggle	kämpfen, sich abmühen

"That's right," laughed Alicia. "I've learnt the perfect method by now – all I have to do is pull her hair and she'll pretend to be interested in maths for five more minutes!"

"Sounds like Holly!" said Daniel.

He and Holly had known each other for a long time, but they had not been close lately because they had started to become interested in different things. Holly sometimes thought that he was a bit of a geek, because he always got good marks at school, while she struggled to even pay attention. But as they chatted that night, Holly began to remember their childhood friendship. Soon the disco was almost over, and it was time to find her friends and go home. She said goodbye to Daniel and Alicia and went to look for Evie, Emily and Nina.

ÜBUNG 12: True or false? Kreuze die richtigen Aussagen an.

1. Holly's dress was long enough to reach her ankles. ❑
2. The four girls met at Emily's house before the dance began. ❑
3. Alicia wanted to dance, but her date Daniel wouldn't dance with her. ❑
4. Holly told Daniel that she had seen him at Evie's football match. ❑
5. Alicia wakes Holly up if she falls asleep in maths. ❑
6. Holly and Daniel stopped being close friends because he was better at school and Holly was jealous. ❑
7. The four girls walked home together in silence. ❑

Once they had all found each other, the best friends started to walk home together, and Holly was happy to listen to the other three girls talking excitedly about everything that had happened that evening. Everyone had had a fantastic time, and as each of them said goodbye before going home to bed, they looked forward to discussing it all again together the next day.

3

Playing the Blues

3

Die vier Mädchen gehen auf Shoppingtour und unterhalten sich über den Vorabend in der Schuldisco. Ihr Plan hat gut funktioniert: Sie haben sich bei der Party alle prächtig amüsiert! Am Nachmittag holt Holly Evie vom Fußballtraining ab. Dort trifft sie Daniel, ihren alten Freund aus Kindertagen. Sie unterhalten sich und tauschen Erinnerungen aus. Evie findet, dass Daniel einen Flirt wert wäre, aber Holly ist da anderer Meinung: Ein netter Kerl, aber nicht besonders aufregend!

The day after the school dance was a Saturday, and the girls decided to go shopping together in the town centre. After over an hour, their conversation was still focused on the night before.

"Oh, I had so much fun last night!" said Emily, picking up a pair of earrings.

"We know," said Evie with smile.

She had already heard all about it several times, but was glad that her friend was so happy. She added, "It looked like Adam did, too. He couldn't stop looking at you all night."

Emily's cheeks went slightly pink. "Actually," she admitted, "at the end of the dance he asked me out on a date with him."

"Why didn't you tell us?!" asked Holly. She always loved to be the first to know about anything to do with love and romance and could not wait to hear more of Emily's news.

"Because I didn't say yes," replied Emily.

Nina looked shocked. "I thought you liked him. You've been spending a lot of time together at school."

"The truth is that although he's good-looking, he's a bit boring sometimes," explained Emily. "He's always talking about himself, but he doesn't really listen to anything that *I* say. Last night he asked me three times how many brothers and sisters I had! And I had already told him last week that I was an only child!"

Holly was surprised. "But you always look like you're having a great time with him at school."

Emily blushed again. "Have you ever noticed that Nathan is usually watching when I speak to Adam?" she asked shyly.

"And you're just trying to make Nathan feel jealous?" Evie guessed. "If it makes you feel any better, when he sees you together, Nathan always does look like he's thinking about going over and punching Adam in the face. He looks completely miserable."

focused on	bezogen auf
only child	Einzelkind
jealous	eifersüchtig
sigh	Seufzer

"Well if Nathan really likes me so much, why didn't he want to go to the dance with me?" asked Emily with a sigh. "Boys are so confusing."

"I don't know," said Holly. "But it's a bit strange that he didn't go with anyone else instead. In fact I don't think I saw him there at all."
"Me neither," said Emily, followed by Evie and Nina, who both repeated the same thing. Nobody had seen him at the disco, not even once.
"Maybe he just really, really hates dancing?" suggested Nina.
"Or pop music," added Evie.
"Or maybe his dog ate his ticket," joked Holly.
"It doesn't matter anyway," said Emily. "I don't want to go out with either of them."

ÜBUNG 13: Synonyms. Finde im Text die Synonyme der folgenden Wörter!

1. a little bit ....
2. confessed ....
3. attractive ....
4. normally ....
5. very unhappy ....
6. puzzling ....
7. weird ....
8. said again ....

Two hours later Holly was ready to go home. Evie had already left to play football with the boys, and Holly realized that their game was about to end. She decided to go to meet Evie, as the sports centre was on her way home.

muddy	schmutzig

When she got there, Daniel waved to her again. This time Holly waved back and walked over to where he was sitting, wearing a muddy Arsenal shirt. He explained that Evie was having a shower and would be ready in a few minutes.

annoying	lästig, nervig
to argue	behaupten, einwenden
water gun	Wasserpistole
bucket	Eimer
changing room	Umkleide
to judge	beurteilen
defensively	verteidigend
straight away	auf Anhieb, sofort

"I hoped I'd see you again soon," he said. "It was really good to talk to you again last night. You aren't nearly as annoying as you were when you were little!"

Holly laughed, but argued, "You were the annoying one! Especially that summer when you bought that huge water gun... you used to hide behind the bushes and shoot me when I walked past your house!"

"Until you ran into my garden and threw a whole bucket of water over me the next day!" he said. "I knew not to upset you from then on!"

"That's right," she said. "And you knew I could always beat you in a fight anyway!"

Daniel started to say something in response, but at that moment Evie came out of the changing room. So Holly quickly said goodbye to Daniel, and the two girls began their walk home together. Evie asked her what she had been talking about with Daniel.

"Oh, just some memories from years ago," Holly answered. "We used to be good friends but I haven't seen him much lately. He's a bit of a geek to be honest."

"A geek?! He's the best in our football team," said Evie, looking surprised.

"Oh Evie, you always judge boys by how good they are at football!" said Holly.

"Well, I think he's nice," said Evie, a little defensively. "We have a lot of fun together at football anyway. And when Alicia was upset because nobody would go to the disco with her, he said straight away that he would take her."
Although Holly knew that she was only interested in Daniel as a friend, she was surprised to find that a small part of her felt glad to hear that he and Alicia were not a couple after all.
"Well, I thought you must like him anyway," said Evie. "I guess you don't."
"Daniel?! No way!" said Holly, "Not like that. I'm sure he's very good at football like you say, but I would never even think about going out with him."

ÜBUNG 14: Match-up. Verbinde die Satzanfänge mit den richtigen Satzenden!

1. ❑ When I was a child, I used to...
2. ❑ Last weekend, I...
3. ❑ At the moment, I...
4. ❑ Next week I am going to...
5. ❑ If I could, I would...

a) go to the beach, if it's hot enough to sunbathe.
b) have a huge crush on a famous actor.
c) like playing with dolls and stuffed toys.
d) buy a hundred pairs of shoes.
e) went to the cinema with two of my best friends.

Evie shrugged, and they carried on walking home as though she had never mentioned Daniel at all.
The next Monday at school, the girls were laughing and joking together during lunch break when they were interrupted by the sound of somebody speaking much more loudly than normal nearby.
"Well of course I'm going to win. No-one around here has any real talent anyway. Most of the performances will be completely pathetic."

Holly looked around to see where the voice was coming from. It was shrill and unpleasant and sounded familiar. She knew exactly whose voice it was as soon as she saw Samantha Lavigne sitting on a bench with two other girls, who were looking right at her and her friends. All three were very pretty, but had a cruel look in their eyes.

to shrug	die Schultern zucken
performance	Auftritt
pathetic	erbärmlich
unpleasant	unangenehm
cruel	gemein

"Did you hear that Holly Brown has entered the contest, too?" Samantha continued.
Holly felt her cheeks grow hot as she heard her own name. Then Samantha and her friends suddenly started to speak much more quietly. Although Holly could not hear what they were saying, she saw their cruel expressions become sharper, before they all laughed even louder than before.
Evie noticed that Holly looked upset.
"Ignore them," she said. "Why don't we go and sit somewhere else?"
They got up and sat on the grass on the other side of the field as Evie had suggested. As soon as they were far enough away not to be heard, Nina said angrily,
"I can't believe some of the things that girl says. She thinks she's so much better than everyone else."
"All three of them think they're so popular and cool. They don't seem to have noticed that nobody in the whole school

fist	Faust
clenched	geballt
clarinet	Klarinette
unfortu-nately	leider
to pour	schütten
ink	Tinte
determined	entschlossen
mess	Durcheinander
anxiously	ängstlich
loads	jede Menge
curious	neugierig

actually likes any of them!" said Evie. She had her fists clenched as though she was thinking about punching Samantha.

Holly put her hand on Evie's shoulder to calm her down. "The problem is that she probably *will* win the talent contest," she said. "I hate the way she talks like she's the queen of the school as well, but I've seen her in music classes and she plays the clarinet really well unfortunately."

"It doesn't seem fair that someone so horrible should have such good luck," said Emily. "She always seems to win everything. And she always has the most expensive clothes and the newest mobile phone."

"Yeah, but it's not just good luck though," added Evie. "Don't you remember the time that she poured ink all over Emily's painting when no-one was looking, just before the art competition?"

"How could I forget?" asked Emily sadly. "I spent hours painting that picture, and she completely ruined it just because she knew it was better than hers."

"Well, we can't let her win this time," said Nina, sounding determined.

"You have to beat her, Holly!" agreed Emily.

Holly remembered her guitar lessons with Matt, and how she had not been able to play more than ten notes without an ugly-sounding mistake. After all, she had only entered the competition as an excuse to see him, so she had almost completely forgotten about it since he left. Now, for the first time, she imagined herself actually on the stage, playing the same mess of wrong notes in front of everybody in the school.

"I can't!" she cried out anxiously.

"Don't be silly, Hol, you practised loads with Matt, you must be really good by now," said Emily.

"And if you just keep practising every day you'll have a real chance of winning," added Evie. "Just keep thinking about how great it would be to see Samantha get what she deserves."

"Yeah, show her how wrong she is when she says all the other performances are going to be pathetic," said Nina. "She'll feel stupid when someone else wins the contest instead of her."

But Holly worried that "pathetic" might be just the right word to describe her performance.

During her last class of the afternoon, Holly was counting every second before the final bell rang to tell everyone that it was time to go home. Running out of the classroom, she suddenly noticed Nathan standing in the corridor on his own. It was the first time that any of the girls had seen him since before the school disco, and Holly felt so curious about where he had been that she decided to go and speak to him.

But when she smiled and said "hi", Nathan barely mumbled a hello, without the slightest hint of a smile in return.

Holly decided not to waste her time talking to him if he was going to be so rude and went to meet her friends outside instead. Once all of them had arrived, Holly told them about Nathan's strange behaviour.

ÜBUNG 15: Unscramble the words! Ordne die Buchstaben zu sinnvollen Wörtern.

1. Samantha Lavigne thinks that she is the most (rapulop) .... girl in the school.
2. She is certain that she is the most (tentlead) .... and will win the talent contest.
3. She always wins school (petomictison) ....
4. Samantha is a great (sacimiun) .... , so it will be difficult to beat her in the contest.
5. But Holly's friends are (tindermeed) .... that this time Samantha must not win.

"I don't know why I ever liked him," said Emily. "He's obviously just a very rude and selfish person."

"At least things didn't get more serious between the two of you before you realized that," said Nina.

"That's why it's best to flirt, but not fall in love!" said Holly.

slightest hint	geringste Andeutung
rude	unhöflich
behaviour	Verhalten
selfish	egoistisch
desperately	verzweifelt
to get sth. exactly right	etw. genau richtig machen
to reassure	versichern

"Definitely," said Emily. "Anyway Holly, why don't you show us your song for the contest... the one that you're going to play when you beat Samantha Lavigne!"

"Um... I haven't quite perfected it yet," said Holly.

As soon as the word "contest" had been mentioned, she had immediately felt hot and anxious. She desperately tried to think of a good excuse so that she would not have to play the guitar in front of them.

"I... I want to get it exactly right before I show you all," she said.

"You don't have to worry about that, Holly," Evie reassured her. "We know it won't be perfect yet, but maybe we could give you some suggestions that will help you make it a bit better."

"Er, no, it's really okay," responded Holly, now feeling even more nervous than before. "I still need to practise some more before it's ready for anyone to hear."

"Well, just let us know when you're ready then," said Nina.

Even her patient words worried Holly. She wondered how much longer she could continue making excuses before everyone would find out her unmelodious secret.

ÜBUNG 16: Odd one out! Welches Wort ist das „schwarze Schaf"?

1. instrument, ball, strings, notes

2. selfish, unkind, rude, pleasant

3. Science, experiments, Maths, French

4. neck, lungs, heart, brain

5. aunt, brother, grandmother, neighbour

Holly felt relieved when she reached her home and no longer had to talk to anyone about the contest. But as soon as she entered her bedroom and saw her guitar, which she had abandoned under a pile of clothes, she felt more hopeless than ever. She felt like she had to get away from the room, where her guitar seemed to stare at her, constantly reminding her of her problem.
Then she had a thought. She knew where she could go to get away from her worries.

As she knocked at the yellow door of a small but pretty house, Holly hoped that her friend was at home.
A few moments later, Daniel opened the door.

patient	geduldig
to abandon	ablegen
pile	Haufen
to stare	anstarren
constantly	ständig
worry	Sorge
to knock	anklopfen

He seemed surprised that Holly had come to see him, but he smiled when he saw her – a smile which seemed to reach every part of his face.

"Hey Dan," she said. "I thought it would be nice to come over to your house, just like old times. But I promise I won't throw any water over you this time!"

Daniel laughed and invited Holly in, and, before long, she was really enjoying herself. They had been talking for a while, when Daniel started telling a story about some of his friends and mentioned Nathan. Holly remembered her earlier confusion, when Nathan had not wanted to speak to her at school.

"Do you know why Nathan didn't go to the dance?" she asked. "He told Emily that he wouldn't go with her, and since then he's been acting strangely."

"Oh, yeah, I think I know why that is," Daniel replied.

"Really?" asked Holly eagerly. She had not expected him to know and was excited to hear the reason for Nathan's mysterious behaviour.

"Well, he's really shy about it, but I guess I can tell you since you'll find out anyway. If he's been acting strangely it's probably because he's embarrassed..."

"Embarrassed about what?!" Holly interrupted. Now she really wanted to know.

"About his new brace. He had to have it put in on Friday at the dentist. He didn't want to go to the dance that night because he didn't want everyone to see. He's actually quite shy, although he doesn't seem it."

Holly suddenly understood. She remembered how Nathan had seemed like he did not

to act strangely	sich merkwürdig verhalten
eagerly	begierig, eifrig
mysterious	geheimnisvoll, rätselhaft
to be embarrassed	verlegen sein, sich schämen
brace	Zahnspange
to avoid	vermeiden

want to smile or speak to her in the corridor at school. And she realized that in fact he had just been trying to avoid opening his mouth and showing her his new brace. Then she remembered all the bad things she and her friends had said about him...

ÜBUNG 17: Match-up. Welche Ausdrücke gehören zusammen?

1.	to act	a dance
2.	slightest	excuses
3.	to tell	relieved
4.	to go to	strangely
5.	to feel	a story
6.	to make	hint

"Poor Nathan! We all thought that he was being rude. He really should have told Emily about it though; she thought he didn't like her when he was actually just nervous about how he looked. I'm sure that isn't important to her."
"That's true," said Daniel, "but sometimes you forget that the people that really care about you won't stop liking you just because of a silly thing like that. It can seem easier to keep the things that make you feel embarrassed secret from even your closest friends."

Talking to Daniel had made Holly feel much more relaxed, but now she was reminded of her problem. His words were the exact mirror of her own situation. She realized that she could not keep it secret any longer.

Daniel listened to Holly as the problem that she had been keeping to herself came flooding out of her mouth almost uncontrollably. She felt much better after she had told him how worried she was about the contest which was now only three weeks away.

Eventually he told her, "That's a difficult situation, but I'm sure there must be a way to make it better. If you really can't play the guitar, it's not too late to change your performance."

"But I don't have any talents! I can't think of anything else I could do at the contest."

to flood out	heraus-sprudeln
uncontroll-ably	unkontrollierbar
gradually	allmählich, nach und nach

"Well, it sounds silly, but I was surprised when you said you were going to play the guitar. I would have thought you would be dancing, since you used to love it so much."

It was true. Holly had always loved to dance, and as a child she had been in a few different dancing clubs. However, she had gradually stopped going to them as she got older.

ÜBUNG 18: Are you a good friend? Kreuze an!

1. Your friend is having a difficult time. What do you do?
   a) ❑ Ask her about it straight away. You want to know all the gossip.
   b) ❑ Ignore it, unless she mentions it herself.
   c) ❑ Try to find a good time to sensitively ask her about her problem.

2. A boy you like asks you on a date but he recently broke up with your friend. What do you do?
   a) ❑ Say yes, of course!
   b) ❑ You would only do it if your friend agreed that it was okay.
   c) ❑ You wouldn't even think about saying yes, because a friend is more important than a date.

3. Your friend lets you borrow her favourite skirt for a party. Unfortunately, someone spills orange juice on it, ruining it completely. What do you do?
   a) ❑ Give it back to her as it is. It wasn't you that spilled the juice on it, anyway.
   b) ❑ Tell her that you are really sorry and that she can borrow any of yours whenever she wants.
   c) ❑ Apologize and buy her a new skirt to replace the other one.

4. You and your friend are auditioning for the same part in a school play. What do you do before the audition?
   a) ❑ Say something to her that will make her more nervous, so that she won't act as well as you.
   b) ❑ Try your hardest and let the director decide which of you deserves the part.
   c) ❑ Tell the director that he should choose your friend, and ask if it is possible to give you a different part in the play.

"It's too late to change it now," Holly said gloomily. "Anyway, thanks a lot for listening to all of my problems, but I should really go now and start practising."

Daniel told her that it had been nice to see her again, and Holly went back to her own home. There she took her guitar out from under a cover of clothes and played the song that she had been practising. But no matter how hard she tried, the sound she made was still just as bad as ever.

gloomily	bedrückt
no matter how	egal wie

4

Love Comes Knocking

4

Nachdem Holly Daniel von ihren Sorgen erzählt hat, geht es ihr viel besser. Doch sie traut sich noch immer nicht, ihren Freundinnen von ihrer Angst vor der Talentshow zu erzählen. Sie möchte sie nicht enttäuschen – und außerdem hat sie es schon so lange hinausgezögert, dass sie nun keinen Mut mehr dazu hat.
Eines Morgens traut Holly ihren Augen nicht: Plötzlich steht Matt vor ihrer Tür! Er könnte ihr helfen, einen leichteren Song für den Wettbewerb auszusuchen – doch Matt hat wenig Interesse daran, Holly bei diesem Problem weiterzuhelfen …

Although telling Daniel about her worries had made Holly feel much better, she still could not find the courage to admit her problem to Emily, Evie or Nina. She had wanted to, but on Tuesday, just as she had been about to tell them, something had stopped her. She had been waiting for them all to join her in the canteen when she heard Samantha do a cruel imitation of Nina's German accent as Nina walked past her. Nina, who was normally the most confident of the group, looked down at the floor and shuffled to Holly's table shyly. But her quietness looked

out of place at the table amongst the angry faces of the other three girls.
"She's such a bully!" said Emily, as frustration flashed through her large, green eyes. "How would she like it if we treated her like that?!"
She spoke loudly enough for Samantha and her two friends to hear her, but they seemed not to notice Emily's words above their own cruel laughter.

imitation	Nachahmung
to shuffle	schlurfen
out of place	fehl am Platz
bully	Rüpel
to flash through	aufblitzen in
nausea	Übelkeit
expectantly	erwartungsvoll
to stutter	stammeln, stottern

"It's okay," said Nina. "They won't be laughing when Holly wins the talent show!"
Holly felt a familiar nausea in her stomach at the mention of the contest. Looking at Nina's determined face, she felt guilty about disappointing her and her other friends, who were all so desperate for her to beat Samantha.
"I meant to tell you all something about that actually," she managed to say.
The others all looked at her expectantly. Holly wished that she had told them sooner, as they all seemed so hopeful now.
"What is it?" asked Nina.
When Holly saw her friends' expressions she suddenly lost all her courage. "Um...," she stuttered, "oh, just that I'm going to practise even more than before. It's about time that someone showed Samantha how wrong she is to think that she's better than everybody else."

Evie, Emily and Nina smiled happily. Holly managed to make her mouth turn up at the edges in what looked to the others like a smile as well. But if they had looked closer, they would have seen the worry in her eyes.

ÜBUNG 19: Correct the text. Unterstreiche im folgenden Textabschnitt die acht falsch geschriebenen Wörter und korrigiere sie!

Holly was worried because she thinked that her performance was going to be the most bad in the whole competition. She did not want to disapoint her friends by let Samantha win, especially after Samantha was unkind at Nina. She wanted to admitted to them that she couldn't play the Guitar as well as they thought, but she losed her courage.

1. .... 5. ....

2. .... 6. ....

3. .... 7. ....

4. .... 8. ....

edge	Ecke
obstacle course	Hindernis-parcours
suspiciously	argwöhnisch
attached	*hier:* angewachsen
puzzled	ratlos, verblüfft

Holly struggled through the rest of the week, thinking up new excuses for not showing her friends the song that she was going to play at the contest. The walk home from school, which was usually her favourite part of the day, suddenly became an obstacle course for Holly. She had to avoid their suggestions with excuses which were becoming more and more difficult to believe. On Thursday she told the girls that she could not play for them because she had lost her guitar. That was when they began to guess that she was hiding something from them.

"Holly, how can you have lost your guitar?" asked Nina suspiciously. "You're going to need it for the contest!"

"Oh, you know what I'm like," Holly replied. "I'd lose my head if it wasn't attached to my body! Anyway, sorry girls, but I've got to go now."

"What?!" said Emily. "What do you mean you've got to go? We haven't reached your house yet!"

"Yeah, I know, but I'm going to run the rest of the way. I don't want to lose any time – I've got to practise as much as I can, after all," Holly replied, and hurried away, leaving the others looking puzzled.

When she reached her street, Holly began to feel bad about all her lies. The problem had got out of control a long time ago. Now keeping it a secret just seemed to create more and more lies.

to exclaim	ausrufen
to owe	schulden
I'd (had) better	ich sollte besser
sing-song	melodisch
delighted	sehr erfreut
skinny	dünn
to light up	erhellen, aufleuchten lassen
genuine	echt, aufrichtig

She walked towards home thinking about her situation, but when she reached it, she did not stop. Instead she sent her mother a text message to tell her that she would be home late. Then she walked on to Daniel's house and knocked on the door.

"You again?!" he exclaimed.

"Well," replied Holly, "before this week I hadn't been round to your house for five years, so I probably owe you a few visits by now."
Inside Daniel's house, she immediately felt more relaxed. For the moment at least, it seemed like she had escaped from the worries that were making her run away from even her closest friends.
As the two of them talked and played computer games together, the minutes soon became hours. Eventually Daniel's mother came to tell them that she was preparing dinner.
"Oh!" said Holly, "I didn't realize it was so late. I'd better go."
"No, no, you don't have to," said Daniel's mother, in a soft, musical accent that Holly remembered well from her childhood. Although Daniel's father was English, his mother came from Brazil. As a little girl Holly had loved her traditional cooking just as much as her sing-song accent. For this reason she was delighted when she heard the words, "Why don't you stay for dinner, Holly?"
"If you're sure that you don't mind, I suppose I could do..." she answered.
"Of course we don't mind!" Daniel's mother said. "And anyway, you're looking too skinny at the moment. You need some good Brazilian food to fill you up!"
Holly looked down at her rather chubby stomach. She knew that she was not looking particularly skinny, but from the warm smile that lit up Daniel's mother's face she could tell that the suggestion was genuine.
"I'd love to!" she replied with a smile.

ÜBUNG 20: National characteristics. Was ist für welches Land typisch? Und wie werden seine Bewohner genannt?

sushi *samba* *spicy food* *frogs' legs*

windmills *Roman history* *bull fighting*

1. Brazil	*Brazilian*	*samba*
2. France	....	....
3.	Italian	....
4. Holland	....	....
5.	Spanish	....
6.	Japanese	....
7. India	....	....

Much later, when she arrived home after a delicious meal, Holly decided to try to solve her problem. She could not play the song that she had chosen, so she looked through her other songbooks to find an easier piece. She managed to play some of them, with one or two mistakes, but when she thought about performing them at the contest, they all seemed much too simple.

An hour later, Holly went to bed. She lay awake for a long time, feeling a knot of worry gradually tighten in her stomach. Eventually she did fall asleep but had a strange dream.

knot	Knoten
to tighten	enger werden
drone	Brummen
abruptly	abrupt, plötzlich
wide awake	hellwach

In the dream she was on the stage at school, playing a song that had only two different notes. She would play one note after another until the sound became one monotonous drone. She saw angry faces watching her. One of them was Samantha Lavigne, who got closer and closer until Holly realized that Samantha was also on the stage, with a huge bottle of ink that she was about to pour all over Holly. Then suddenly, Matt appeared on the stage, too, and pulled Samantha away. He kissed Holly, then took the guitar and began to play a beautiful song. The song made all of the angry faces disappear.

Holly woke up abruptly. She felt confused but wide awake. When she saw the date on her alarm clock she realized with disappointment that the school week still had not finished. She put her covers back over her head and tried to hide from another day of excuses.

On Saturday morning, Holly was in bed thinking about how much she had looked forward to the weekend. Now that it was here, she realized that it only meant another week gone before she would have to perform. She only had two weeks left now.

to tidy one's hair	seine Haare richten/ordnen
speechless	sprachlos

When Holly had finally got up, had a shower and got dressed, she was surprised when her mother told her that there was someone waiting at the door to see her. She wondered if it was Daniel.

Holly walked downstairs, tidying her messy brown hair. What she saw through the half-open door left her speechless.

"Hello, Holly Dolly!" said Matt.

ÜBUNG 21: Falling in love. In welchen Jungentyp würdest du dich verlieben?

1. If you imagine your perfect boyfriend, what is your favourite thing about him?
   a) ❑ The way he looks – he has a handsome face, nice hair and great style.
   b) ❑ The way he treats me – he is always kind, and tells me that I look beautiful every day.
   c) ❑ The fact that he likes the same things as me – I can talk to him about anything and we laugh a lot.

2. What type of clothes would you like best on a boy?
   a) ❑ He has to look cool and trendy.
   b) ❑ I don't really mind what he wears.
   c) ❑ He should wear a jumper with the name of my favourite band on it.

3. If your boyfriend was meeting your friends or family for the first time, how should he act?
   a) ❑ I'd want him to make sure that my friends are all jealous of me!
   b) ❑ I'd like him to show them how much he cares about me.
   c) ❑ He should just be himself. I would hope that they liked him and that he liked *them*, too.

4. What would be the perfect present that a boyfriend could give you?
   a) ❑ Expensive jewellery.
   b) ❑ Red roses.
   c) ❑ Our favourite film on DVD so we can watch it together.
5. Which type of famous person would you be most likely to have a crush on?
   a) ❑ A famous Hollywood actor.
   b) ❑ I don't usually have crushes on famous people.
   c) ❑ A comedian or someone in a band.

Holly closed her eyes and opened them again to make sure that she was not still dreaming. But Matt was still right there in front of her, smiling and waiting for her to say hello.

"What are you doing here?" asked Holly, finally remembering to speak.

"That's not a very nice way to greet me after so long without me!" replied Matt, playfully.

"Sorry," stuttered Holly. "I'm just really surprised to see you."

"I know," he said. "I'm only joking. I hoped that it would be a big surprise."

"Well, it is *quite* surprising," Holly responded. She still could not stop her mouth from hanging open in shock.

to recognize	wieder-erkennen
butterfly	Schmetterling
to pound	heftig schlagen
deep-fried	frittiert
chocolate bar	Schokoriegel

"The truth is that I'm only going to be in town for the weekend," Matt explained. "It's my aunt's birthday, so we've all come down from Scotland to visit. We're leaving tomorrow morning... But I wanted to see you first."

Holly tried to stop herself from feeling the same excitement and happiness that she recognized from months before. Spending time with Matt had always made her heart beat fast and her stomach feel full of butterflies, but she had hoped that her feelings had changed after he had upset her so much. Now her heart was pounding faster than ever.

"I can't believe it's really you," she said. "Come inside."

She took Matt into the living room, and they began to talk about all the things that had happened since they last saw each other.

"Glasgow is pretty cool," said Matt. "I met some other guys that like playing music at school, and now I'm in a new band. The stuff I'm playing at the moment is really different to all that pop music that I used to like. The others would really laugh if I played 'Never Say Never' at band practice now."

"Well I'd be quite happy to never hear that song again either," said Holly, thinking about the contest.

"And you'd never guess some of the things they eat there," Matt added. "Like deep-fried chocolate bars!"

"Really?" asked Holly. "That sounds like the unhealthiest thing I can possibly imagine."

"Yeah, it's delicious!" said Matt. "Anyway, how have you been?"

"Well, I've been okay. But I'm getting worried about the talent contest that I entered. Do you remember?"

"How could I forget, Hol? I've never heard anyone play the guitar... uh, quite so... interestingly as you."

"Very funny," said Holly sarcastically. "But maybe you could help me with it while you're here. I've been thinking of changing the song that I'm going to perform, and I need some advice about which one to choose."

Matt agreed to help her, and Holly brought her guitar into the living room so that they could practise together. First, Matt played her some of the new songs that he had learned in Scotland. His blonde hair fell over his eyes, and he looked just as attractive as she had remembered.

When it was Holly's turn to play, Matt tried to be patient with her but found himself commenting on every mistake.

"Don't do it like that," he said, trying to mask his frustration as she played the wrong note for the third time in a row.

Holly sighed. "Oh, it's hopeless. I really wish I had never entered this contest. Everyone is just going to laugh at me."

"It's okay," said Matt reassuringly. "I'm sure you'll learn it in the end. And anyway, you aren't really that bad."

Even though he had meant it kindly, Matt could not stop it from sounding like a lie.

unhealthy	ungesund
to comment on	sich äußern zu
to mask	verbergen
in a row	in Folge
reassuringly	beruhigend

"You don't have to pretend, I know I'm terrible," she said. "I just don't know what to do about it. My friend said that maybe I should change the whole performance and learn a dance instead."

"A dance?" Matt asked, looking amused by the idea. "I thought the idea was to *stop* this from ending in everyone laughing at you."

ballet routine	Ballettnummer
harshly	barsch

"What's so funny about dancing?"

"Oh come on, Holly. Are you really going to get up there on stage and do a little ballet routine in front of everyone? Grow up."

Holly looked at Matt. He was very good-looking, but now she noticed an arrogant expression that she had not seen before. Holly suddenly felt defensive. She loved dancing and did not like to hear him talk about it so harshly. But she decided not to argue, and so she sat there without speaking and listened to Matt play the guitar.

ÜBUNG 22: Right order. Bringe die folgenden Ereignisse in die richtige Reihenfolge!

a) Holly is shocked to see Matt outside her door.

b) Holly plays the guitar badly, and Matt gets frustrated.

c) Holly asks Matt for some help choosing a new song to learn for the talent contest.

d) When Holly mentions Daniel's suggestion of performing a dance, Matt says something cruel to her.

e) Matt talks about his new band in Glasgow.

f) Matt plays the guitar, while Holly sits next to him.

g) Matt explains the reasons for his visit and when he is planning to leave.

1	2	3	4	5	6	7

A little while later, Matt told Holly that he had to go to his aunt's birthday party, but that he could come back in the evening to see her again. Suddenly his expression became more serious.

"Look," he said, "before I go, I just wanted to say something."

Holly waited, wondering if he was going to explain why he had not replied to any of the e-mails that she had sent to him since he had left.

"I want you to be my girlfriend," he said.

Holly still did not say anything. She was too shocked by everything that had happened that day to know how to respond.

"I made a big mistake when I said that we couldn't carry on seeing each other. I've really missed you, Holly."

Holly's heart started to beat faster again as she absorbed Matt's romantic words. She had been so convinced that he had forgotten all about her. And now here he was, telling her that he still wanted to be with her. During the weeks that he had been gone, she had wished many times that this would somehow happen to her. However, she had never quite believed that it really could. In each of those happy daydreams, Holly had felt so good being with him again and knowing that he had not forgotten her. But somehow that did not match her feelings now.

convinced	überzeugt
to match	passen zu

"I still don't understand though," she said. "I wrote you loads of e-mails and you never replied. You didn't call me or even send me a single text message."

"You know how it is," Matt replied. "I've been really busy. Moving house and making new friends doesn't leave you with much spare time."

to move house	umziehen
irritation	Verärgerung

"In two whole months?!"

"Well, if you're going to be like that, I'll just go now," he said, with a note of irritation in his voice. "You can think about it and let me know."

Matt gave her a quick kiss and left. The kiss was not how she had imagined it would be in her daydreams either, just like the empty feeling that it left inside her.

ÜBUNG 23: True or false? Markiere mit ✔ oder – !

1. Holly is pleased that Matt wants to go out with her, because it means that he had not forgotten about her. ❑
2. Holly is confused when Matt asks her to be his girlfriend, because he had not replied to her mails. ❑
3. Matt becomes irritated when Holly asks him why he did not write to her. ❑
4. Matt didn't have any time to call Holly, he was too busy with homework from his new school. ❑
5. Holly had wished many times that Matt would come back and tell her that he still cares about her. ❑
6. Holly can't wait to tell Emily, Evie and Nina her problem. Her best friends will surely know an easy solution. ❑
7. Holly feels uncomfortable in Daniel's house, because she doesn't like his mother. ❑

In the end it did not take Holly long to reach her decision. She did not feel like she needed to see Matt again, so she just called him in the evening to tell him that she did not want to be his girlfriend. On the other end of the phone, Matt seemed distant but did not argue with her.

Holly lay on her bed thinking about what had happened that day. She thought about Matt, and how different he seemed now, how much less like the Matt that she had imagined. She wondered whether she had also imagined a lot of the things that she liked about him during the time they had been dating.

distant	distanziert
infatuation	Verliebtheit

Then, as she looked around her room, Holly saw her guitar which she had brought back upstairs after Matt had finished playing it. She remembered how all those months ago she had only wanted to learn it so that she could be with him.

She wondered whether the guitar might be just as wrong for her as Matt was.

In that moment, looking at the guitar which so reminded her of her old infatuation with Matt, Holly realized: her reasons for learning how to play the guitar had been all wrong. Perhaps that was why even now she could not make the music that she played on it sound right either.

ÜBUNG 24: Comparative or superlative? Vervollständige die Sätze mit der richtigen Steigerungsform!

1. Emily always got *(good)* .... marks than the other girls in Maths.
2. Holly wants to choose a different song which will be *(easy)* .... for her to perform.
3. At school, Holly finds her daydreams much *(interesting)* .... than what her teachers say.
4. Holly is worried that her performance will be the *(bad)* .... in the contest.
5. Matt lives much *(far)* .... away from Holly now that he has moved to Scotland.
6. Matt seems very different now, much *(little)* .... like the Matt that she had imagined.
7. Nina is the *(confident)* .... one of Holly's friends.

Holly knew then that she should not play the guitar at the talent contest. And she did not need to think for long about what to do instead.

5

Facing the Music

5

Holly hat eine Entscheidung getroffen: Sie hängt die Gitarre endgültig an den Nagel und will nun beim Talentwettbewerb das machen, was sie wirklich gut kann – sie möchte tanzen! Daniel erweist sich als echter Freund. Er spielt ihr brasilianische Musik vor und zeigt ihr die Samba-Grundschritte.
Am Tag des Wettbewerbs ist Holly ziemlich aufgeregt. Sie ist als Letzte an der Reihe und ihr Lampenfieber steigt von Minute zu Minute. Doch als sie schließlich aufgerufen wird und die Musik ansetzt, ist ihre Aufregung mit einem Mal verflogen …

Daniel opened the door and let Holly in – for the third time that week. But this time her face had a very different expression to the look of worry that Holly usually had when she came to see him.
"Dan!" Holly exclaimed. Her face was decorated by a wide, excited smile. "Guess what! I've decided that I do want to dance at the talent show."
"That's great!" said Daniel. "I remember you being a really good dancer even when you were little. And I think it's best to do something that you love."

"I think so, too," she agreed. "And even if I'm not the best performer at the contest, at least I'll be doing something that I feel comfortable with."

"What type of dance are you going to do?" Daniel asked her.

"I don't know yet," she replied. "I only have two weeks to practise a routine, but I don't really remember any from dance classes. I stopped going to them a year ago."

Daniel paused for a minute to think. Then he said, "Well, it sounds silly, but maybe my mum could help you. She's always dancing – she says it reminds her of home. I don't think she knows any dances apart from the samba, though."

"That's a Brazilian dance, right?" asked Holly.

Daniel nodded. "I can show you, if you promise not to laugh of course!"

"I didn't know you could dance!" she said.

"My mum thinks it's important to teach me her family's traditions, so she taught me how to dance the samba when I was really young," Daniel explained. "I don't do it anymore though. And I'm not very good."

"Show me!" said Holly. "I'm sure I won't laugh. There's no way you'll dance half as badly as I play the guitar, anyway. I'll show you that one day if you want to see something that's *really* funny!"

ϟ Guess what!	Stell dir vor!
performer	Darsteller(in)
to feel comfortable	sich wohlfühlen

"It's a deal!" said Daniel. "I'll have to find the right music first though."
He quickly searched through his parents' music collection, before pulling out a brightly-coloured CD. Holly could not read the foreign words on the cover.
When the music started, it was like nothing that Holly had ever heard before. She immediately felt transported to a different, more exotic place, as the beat of drums filled her heart with an unusual melody. Her whole body wanted to move to its rhythm.
She was so distracted by the music that at first she almost forgot to watch Daniel. But when she looked up at him, the way that he was dancing left her equally surprised. He was moving to the music's powerful rhythm just like she wanted to.
"You have to teach me how to do that! It's incredible!"
Daniel stopped dancing and smiled shyly. "Those were just the basic steps really." He turned the music off. "Thanks, though." Holly suspected that he was blushing slightly.
"I'm serious," she insisted. "I want to dance like that in the contest."
"Uh... well, I can show you how if you really want to," he said.
To teach her the dance, Daniel had to hold her close. It made Holly feel quite strange. She only thought of him as a friend, but the touch of his arm around her waist made her stomach flip. She tried not to think about that unexpected feeling and concentrated hard on moving her feet in the right way.

It did not take her very long to learn the moves, and they were soon dancing together as though they had been dance partners for years.
Outside it was getting dark. The last pink streaks of the sunset were disappearing from the sky as darkness covered the street. Holly realized that it was time for her to go home.
She felt extremely confused as she walked the short distance between Daniel's house and her own. Why had this afternoon made her feel differently about her old friend? Her skin tingled with the memory of his arm around her. Holly shook her head, as though trying to shake loose all of her confusing thoughts. That was not how she was supposed to feel about Daniel. He was just a friend. When she arrived home, she saw a letter on the floor by the door. It had no address; on its envelope there was just one word, written in large pink letters: "Holly".

It's a deal!	Abgemacht!
to feel transported to	sich versetzt fühlen nach
beat	Rhythmus, Takt
drum	Trommel, Schlagzeug
equally	gleichermaßen
to suspect	vermuten
to insist	beharren
unexpected	unerwartet
move	Bewegung
streak	Strahl
sunset	Sonnenuntergang
to tingle	prickeln
to shake loose	abschütteln
to rip sth. open	etw. aufreißen

Holly ran up to her room with the mysterious letter. She ripped it open and started to read:

audience	Publikum
to support s.o.	jmd. unterstützen
either way	so oder so

Dear Holly,

We've noticed you haven't seemed like yourself lately. We're your friends and we're all worried, because you haven't spoken to us properly for a while. You seem stressed about the contest, and we just want you to know that you can talk to any of us about it whenever you need to. We hope you know that it really doesn't matter whether you win or lose – it's all the same to us because we'll be there in the audience supporting you just as much either way.

All our love,
Evie, Nina and Emily.

ÜBUNG 25: Answer the questions! Kreuze jeweils die richtige Antwort an.

1. How long did it take Holly to learn how to dance the samba?
   a) ❑ She already knew how, so she didn't have to learn.
   b) ❑ It was too difficult, so she didn't learn it fully.
   c) ❑ Soon after Daniel had shown her how to do it.

2. How does dancing with Daniel make her feel?
   a) ❑ Wonderful. She loves feeling him so close.
   b) ❑ Confused. She likes it, but does not know why.
   c) ❑ Horrible. She finds it strange having to dance so close to him.

3. Why is Daniel able to help Holly learn a new dance routine?
   a) ❑ His parents are Brazilian, and the family have a traditional dancing style which they all know.
   b) ❑ He went to dance classes when he was a child.
   c) ❑ He was taught how to dance the samba by his Brazilian mother when he was a child.

one by one	der Reihe nach
ages ago	vor Ewigkeiten
ϟ to fancy sb.	auf jmd. stehen
to change the subject	das Thema wechseln

Holly put her hand to her mouth as she read their kind words. She wished she had just been honest with them from the start and told them all of her worries and fears. But she was sure that it was not too late to put everything right.

One by one, she called up each of her three best friends and explained all the things that she had been too embarrassed to tell them before.

"But you could have told us that ages ago," said Evie on the telephone when Holly told her what had been worrying her. Holly had been acting so strangely that Evie had expected her problem to be much larger. "You're so silly sometimes, Holly!" she added affectionately.

"I know," Holly replied. "I wish I had told you. But it's okay now anyway – I'm going to dance instead of play the guitar, and I feel much better about the contest already. Dan showed me how to..."

Evie interrupted her. "Oh, I see! Dan... he's that boy who's *definitely* just a friend, right?!" She laughed.

"Yes, that is right actually," said Holly, although this time she felt a little less convinced herself. "He's just a good dancer. I don't... you know... fancy him or anything."

Evie laughed again. "Yeah, I believe you..."

ÜBUNG 26: Opposites. Finde die Gegenteile im Text und schreibe sie auf!

1. relaxed ....
2. worse ....
3. normally ....
4. different ....
5. smaller ....
6. clever ....
7. closed ....
8. enemies ....

Holly tried to ignore Evie's comment. She wasn't sure if she believed the words herself, even though they had come out of her own mouth.

"Well anyway, I promise I'll never let such a stupid thing get in the way of our friendship again," she said, changing the subject. "No more secrets from now on."

"That's right!" said Evie.

Holly could barely wait to see her friends at school the next Monday. On Monday morning she jumped out of bed. She felt more eager to begin the day than she had been feeling in weeks.

Over the next week and a half Holly spent many happy hours with her best friends, but she also went to Daniel's house more than ever. She practised her dance routine with him almost every day. When she remembered how difficult it had been to improve her guitar playing, she could not believe how much progress she had made in her dancing in just two short weeks.

"Wow, Holly," said Daniel as she finally collapsed on the sofa after an hour's energetic dancing. "You're really good at this!"

"I love it!" Holly said, smiling brightly. She was tired, but her skin was glowing with happiness. "I just feel so much better dancing than playing the guitar. I don't know why, but playing the guitar never felt natural to me."

"Well, you are definitely a natural dancer," said Daniel. "Samantha hasn't got a chance!"

"You haven't seen her play. She's the best at music in the whole school. She plays the clarinet so well... I guess she deserves to win."

Daniel looked shocked.

"Wait a minute, are you sure you're alright?" he asked her. "Did you hit your head on something while you were dancing and get amnesia?"

Holly laughed. "Well okay, she doesn't deserve to win, but she probably will do anyway."

"Well, I'll be right at the front of the crowd cheering for you anyway. Maybe I'll make a banner!" said Daniel jokingly.

Holly turned away from him and thought for a moment. Her best friends would be at the front of the crowd, too, and Evie already thought that she liked Daniel. She suddenly felt hot and embarrassed. Her mind filled with things that she knew should not really matter, like the fact that he often wore unusual clothes or read odd-looking books – things which made her worry about what people would think when they saw him cheering for her.

progress	Fortschritt
to collapse	zusammenbrechen
energetic	schwungvoll
to glow	glühen
natural dancer	geborene(r) Tänzer(in)

"Listen," Holly finally said. "I'd prefer it if you didn't do that really... I just... don't want it to seem like I've been telling everyone to cheer for me. I'd prefer it if you sat further back and weren't too loud."

Daniel looked a bit hurt. He seemed to guess why she did not want his support to be too obvious.

"No banner either then?" he joked.

"No!" she said, a bit too loudly.

"Okay then..." Daniel agreed.

crowd	Menge
to cheer for sb.	jdn. anfeuern, Beifall klatschen
banner	Transparent, Spruchband
odd-looking	sonderbar aussehend

ÜBUNG 27: Short forms. Vervollständige die Sätze mit der Kurzform!

1. Holly *(can not)* .... wait to see her friends at school.
2. *(She is)* .... feeling much happier now that she *(is not)* .... keeping any secrets from them anymore.
3. Daniel thinks that Samantha *(has not)* .... got a chance of beating Holly. He thinks *(she will)* .... win the contest with her performance.
4. Holly *(does not)* .... agree. She thinks *(he is)* .... forgetting how good Samantha is at playing the clarinet.
5. Holly says *(she would)* .... prefer it if Daniel *(did not)* .... cheer loudly for her or sit close to the stage.
6. Daniel tells her that he *(will not)* .... sit at the front if she (does not) .... want him to.

full volume	volle Lautstärke
to scold	(aus)schimpfen
effort	Anstrengung
to stay still	still halten

With just two days to go before the contest, Holly tried to practise as much as possible. She danced in her room alone with her music playing at full volume. She danced while she brushed her teeth. She danced all through the kitchen, while her mother scolded her for getting in the way of her cooking.

The talent show was on a Friday afternoon, and it had been decided that all of the school were going to miss their last two classes to attend it. By that time, Holly was so used to dancing everywhere that it took some effort for her to stay still during her lessons that morning. By the time the afternoon arrived, she was feeling nervous but ready.

The first performance was by a blonde girl called Lydia. She was one of Samantha Lavigne's friends, and almost as talented as Samantha. She played a piece of classical music on the violin which made Holly feel suddenly much less confident. The next performance did not help either – Alicia sounded like an angel as she flawlessly sang a solo piece. Holly was going to be the last to go on stage, and so she had to watch as each performer left to a storm of applause from the audience. There were only two other dance acts, and both were groups who had chosen to dance to pop music, in a completely different style to Holly's unusual samba.

flawlessly	fehlerlos
act	Darbietung
to bow	sich verbeugen
surrounded by	umgeben von
to trip	stolpern
to tremble	zittern
to pulse	pulsieren

Frightening images from her dream began to come back into Holly's mind without warning. She remembered seeing herself on the stage, playing terribly, in front of all of those angry faces...

I can't do it! Holly thought. All that she could think about was running away from the school, and from the terrifying moment when she would have to perform in front of everyone. But she felt even worse a minute later when Samantha confidently walked onto the stage and began playing her clarinet. She had chosen a very complicated song, but did not make any mistakes, and looked extremely pleased with herself as she bowed and left the stage. Now there was only one more performance left. There was no time to run away.

Holly walked onto the stage nervously. She felt very small, surrounded by so much space and so many people all waiting for her to begin. She tripped over a cable that had been left behind when they had taken away a microphone, and even in such a large crowd she was sure that she recognized the cruel laugh that came from nearby: it could only be Samantha's.

electric current	elektrischer Strom
to cheer	jubeln
to stand out from	sich abheben von

But as soon as the music began, all of the fear that had made Holly tremble and sweat just moments before turned into energy. The rhythm of the music pulsed through her like an electric current, and her body seemed to move without her even thinking about the steps.

She knew the dance so well, and danced it so naturally, that she hardly noticed time passing and had soon reached the end of her performance. As she threw her arms to her sides in the final position of the dance, the whole audience cheered. It was only then that she was able to see their faces – they looked very different to the angry ones that she had imagined in her dream. Instead, all of the faces in front of her now were smiling and cheering. Three faces in particular stood out from the rest. Nina, Evie and Emily were right at the front, cheering louder than anyone else in the room.

ÜBUNG 28: Match-up. Verbinde die Satzanfänge mit den richtigen Satzenden!

1. ❑ Holly danced all over the house...
2. ❑ Samantha was very pleased with her own performance...
3. ❑ Holly felt worse about her own performance...
4. ❑ Holly was not the only person who had chosen to dance in the contest...
5. ❑ Watching the other performers and seeing the audience's response...

a) but all of the others were dancing to pop music.
b) when she heard Lydia and Alicia perform so well.
c) because she had not made a single mistake.
d) made Holly feel even more nervous.
e) in preparation for her dance performance.

A few minutes later, after the judges had all voted, the room became unusually quiet as everybody waited to hear who had won. The runner's up prize went to Alicia, who looked shocked but very happy when her name was called. She could not stop smiling as she collected her prize. Then, moments later, one of the judges began to speak again.

judge	Juror
to vote	abstimmen, bewerten
runner's up prize	zweiter Preis
to collect	abholen

"But now I am pleased to tell you that the winner of this year's talent contest is..."
Holly looked at Samantha. Samantha seemed to be getting ready to go back on the stage to collect the winner's prize. She was just waiting to hear the two words that she was sure would follow: Samantha Lavigne.
"Holly Brown!" said the loud voice of the judge.
Holly looked around her as though she was checking to see if there were any other girls called Holly Brown anywhere nearby. Then she screamed with delight as she realized that she really had won the contest.

delight	Freude, Entzücken
trophy	Pokal
to reappear	wieder auftauchen
weird	eigenartig, schräg

When Holly came back down from the stage carrying her trophy and prize money, Nina, Emily and Evie all ran up to her. For a second, Holly thought she saw Daniel far away in the crowd, before the girls all gave her a huge hug. Before long it was hard to see where Holly had disappeared to amongst all of the arms that were covering her. She was still smiling when she reappeared, but she could not help but feel that something was not quite right.
"I know this sounds weird," she said, "but I think I have to go. I'll be back in five minutes, okay?" The others all looked at each other and laughed. Evie, especially, did not look at all surprised. Holly ran to the back of the room, and put her hand on Daniel's shoulder. He turned around.

ÜBUNG 29: Prepositions. Unterstreiche die richtige Präposition!

1. Holly learned her dance routine in/at Daniel's house.
2. Holly only practiced her dance routine for/during two weeks.
3. Samantha was very happy with/by her performance, but it was not good enough for/to win the contest.
4. Holly felt very nervous about performing behind/in front of so many people.
5. Now the judges are going to give a prize for/to Holly for/from winning the talent contest.

"Have you come to tell me off?" he asked with a mischievous grin. "I tried really hard not to cheer for you, honestly! And I only clapped a *little* bit!"

"No, don't be silly!" Holly laughed. "I don't know why I ever said any of that. You should have been at the front, I don't know what I was thinking when I told you to stand further back. Without you I wouldn't have been able to do that dance at all... so... I want you to have this."

Holly held out her arm. A silver envelope containing all the prize money that she had just won shimmered in her hand.

to tell sb. off	jdn. ausschimpfen
mischievous	verschmitzt, spitzbübisch
to clap	klatschen
to shimmer	schimmern
grateful	dankbar
throat	Hals, Kehle

"No, Holly, you won it by yourself," Daniel told her. "I couldn't take it."

"But I want you to know how grateful I am. Actually... Dan, what I really want you to know is how important you are to me. I..." Holly tried to stop, but the rest of the sentence was burning in the back of her throat.

"I love you."

As soon as the words escaped Holly wanted to grab them out of the air and put them right back where they had come from. Without thinking she took a step backwards, away from Daniel.

to head towards home	heimwärts steuern

"Uh... I'd better go," she said. "Don't say anything. You don't have to say anything."
Daniel stepped towards her and put his finger over her mouth gently.
"It's okay," he said, "you have no idea how long I've felt that way about you. I love you, too, Holly."

The next week, Holly and her best friends were beginning their walk back from school just as they had done hundreds of times before, smiling as they left the school gates and headed towards home.
"Do you have any plans for tonight, Holly?" asked Nina.
"Nothing special," Holly replied. "I'm going to Dan's house this evening though, for dinner and dancing."
"Ooh, you're going to your *boyfriend's* house," Evie joked in a childish voice.

ÜBUNG 30: The right boyfriend? Finde heraus, ob du und dein Freund füreinander bestimmt seid!

1. When you think about him, how do you feel?
   a) ❑ I get butterflies in my stomach, and I feel warm and happy inside. *(8 points)*
   b) ❑ No different to how I feel when I think about other things. *(0 points)*
   a) ❑ I start smiling for no reason, even when I'm doing something really boring. *(4 points)*

2. How similar are the two of you?
   a) ❑ We like the same things and agree about almost everything. *(8 points)*
   b) ❑ Quite similar, but sometimes it's difficult to decide what we do together, but usually we find something we both enjoy. *(4 points)*
   c) ❑ We're very different to each other, but we still find things to talk about. *(0 points)*

3. If you imagine yourself two years from now, can you see you and him still being together?
   a) ❑ No, definitely not. I don't think that we will still know each other anymore by then. *(0 points)*
   b) ❑ I would really like us to still be together, but it's impossible to say what will happen. *(3 points)*
   c) ❑ Absolutely. I can't imagine life without him. *(7 points)*

4. What do your friends and family think of him?
   a) ❑ They love him! My best friends think that we are the perfect couple. *(7 points)*
   b) ❑ We have the same friends, so they must like him! My family seem to get on well with him, too. *(3 points)*
   c) ❑ They don't know him. I haven't introduced him to my friends or family. *(0 points)*

"*Yes*, Evie!" replied Holly, pretending to be annoyed. "I'm going to my boyfriend's house! Surely this shouldn't be fun for you anymore, now that I've admitted that Dan and I are together!"

to be mad at sb.	auf jmd. wütend sein
shade	Farbton, Abtönung
deep scarlet	scharlachrot
to overcome	überwinden
despite	trotz

They all laughed.

"But I do feel bad about not telling you all about Dan earlier," said Holly, more seriously now. "I'm really sorry for breaking our rule... you know... flirt, but don't fall in love."

The others didn't laugh this time. Instead there was a strange silence in the air, and the other three all looked down at their feet at the same time. Holly was confused.

"So, you aren't mad at me then?" she asked.

"Well... no," said Emily.

As she looked up Holly could see that her cheeks had gone a little pink.

"I couldn't really be angry about that. I meant to tell you something as well... I've started going out with Nathan again."

The others all asked her questions at once, and the pink shade of Emily's cheeks soon turned into a deep scarlet. She explained everything, telling them how Nathan had overcome his shyness about his new brace. And how he had asked her whether despite his behaviour for the last few weeks she would still be interested in going on a date with him. Emily seemed very happy that they were back together.

confession	Geständnis
to fall for sb.	in jdn. verknallt sein
to regret sth.	etw. bedauern
blossom	Blüte

Now it was Nina's turn to make a confession.

"I thought I was the one who was breaking our promise, because I really like Kieran. I'm really falling for him..."

"...And I can't stop thinking about Ben!" said Evie loudly, surprising everyone.

"Hey!" said Holly. "We don't even know who he is!"

"Well, my secret must be the best one then!" Evie exclaimed. "I could have guessed all of yours easily to be honest."

"Go on then, explain everything!" said Nina excitedly.

"Ben's not from our school," began Evie, "I met him at the tennis club. He's really good at sport..."

As they turned the corner and continued down the street towards their homes no-one regretted breaking the promise that they had made all those weeks ago. The days were beginning to get sunnier, and pink blossoms decorated the trees all along the road. It already seemed a long time ago that they had decided not to fall in love. Now the feelings that had led them to that decision also seemed distant.

Holly thought about everything that had happened to her in the last few months and felt lucky to now have a boyfriend who had made her change her mind about all of her ideas of love. Now she did not need to daydream anymore. Most of all though, she felt happy to be with her three best friends in the world – and that was one thing that would never change.

Lösungen & Glossar

Lösungen

ÜBUNG 1:

1. falsch 2. falsch 3. richtig 4. falsch 5. falsch

ÜBUNG 2:

Mostly a): You put a lot of effort into your appearance and always look good, but you should only spend a lot of time doing this if it makes you happy. Remember that beauty comes from the inside, and your friends and family love you for who you are and not for what you look like.

Mostly b): Your ideas about fashion are very sensible. You look good, but you know that there are more important things than clothes. Well done! Don't be afraid to try out new styles sometimes as well, though.

Mostly c): Fashion is not very important to you, and you don't like shopping. If you put a bit more effort into choosing clothes, you might be surprised by the results. However as long as you feel good about yourself there is no need to change.

ÜBUNG 3:

1. chubby 2. flattering 3. crush 4. overheard 5. burst 6. blushed 7. horrified

ÜBUNG 4:

1. falsch 2. falsch 3. richtig

ÜBUNG 5:

1. a 2. b 3. c

ÜBUNG 6:

1. Maths 2. friends 3. box 4. swimming 5. clock 6. journey 7. secret

Lösung: anxious

ÜBUNG 7:

1. d 2. a 3. f 4. c 5. e 6. b

ÜBUNG 8:

1. Each of the four girls brought her favourite film and a dessert to the sleepover. It was at Nina's house.
2. Holly is reminded of Matt when she watches a love film with a sad ending.
3. Evie and Nina do not agree about whether Holly should try to forget about Matt: Evie thinks that she should forget about him and move on, but Nina thinks that it is worth staying in touch with him. However, Nina changes her mind.
4. The fact that Matt never replies to Holly's emails or text messages makes it hard for her to stay friends with him.
5. They guess that Emily might be upset because she has been unusually quiet. She has her hair over her face and is not looking very happy.
6. Holly ate two enormous bowls of ice cream.

ÜBUNG 9:

1. thought 2. forget 3. decided 4. went

ÜBUNG 10:

1. mashed potatoes 2. quiz show 3. sunrise 4. grass 5. rival 6. dog

ÜBUNG 11:

4–8 points: You don't flirt much at all, but not because you don't know how – just because you don't want to. You have better things to do and to think about, and as a result you are an interesting person to talk to. You may find that this makes boys like you much more than if you just flirted with them!

9–15 points: You are quite shy, and you often feel nervous around boys. However, your sweet personality and your modesty mean that you probably have more secret admirers than you think. Be brave and talk to the boy that you like today!

16–22 points: You're a total flirt! You love boys, and there are always plenty of them around you, as they are attracted by the way you dress and your flirting style. However, you need to be careful that you don't ignore your friends or upset them – boyfriends come and go, but friends are forever.

ÜBUNG 12:

1. falsch 2. richtig 3. falsch 4. falsch 5. richtig 6. falsch 7. falsch

ÜBUNG 13:

1. slightly 2. admitted 3. good-looking 4. usually 5. miserable 6. confusing 7. strange 8. repeated

ÜBUNG 14:

1. c 2. e 3. b 4. a 5. d

ÜBUNG 15:

1. popular 2. talented 3. competitions 4. musician 5. determined

ÜBUNG 16:

1. ball 2. pleasant 3. experiments 4. neck 5. neighbour

ÜBUNG 17:

1. act strangely 2. slightest hint 3. tell a story 4. go to a dance 5. feel relieved 6. make excuses

ÜBUNG 18:

Mostly a): You are not a good friend because you care more about yourself than you do about other people. You should try to think about how you treat your friends in future, because if you continue the way you are now, soon you might not have many left.

Mostly b): You are a good friend, and you are good at keeping a balance between treating your friends kindly and not missing out on what you want for yourself. There are small ways in which you could be slightly more thoughtful at times, but you are certainly a friend worth having!

Mostly c): You are the type of friend that everybody wants to have. You are always nice to people, and that wins you lots of friends who really love you for who you are. It can also attract people who want to get something from you though, so make sure that you remember to be kind to yourself as well as to others.

ÜBUNG 19:

1. thinked (thought) 2. most bad (worst) 3. disapoint (disappoint) 4. by let (by letting) 5. unkind at (unkind to) 6. wanted to admitted (wanted to admit) 7. Guitar (guitar) 8. losed (lost)

ÜBUNG 20:

1. Brazil, Brazilian, samba
2. France, French, frogs' legs
3. Italy, Italian, Roman history
4. Holland, Dutch, windmills
5. Spain, Spanish, bull fighting
6. Japan, Japanese, Sushi
7. India, Indian, spicy food

ÜBUNG 21:

Mostly a): You sometimes focus a bit too much on looks, which can lead you to fall in love with boys who won't treat you very nicely or who simply aren't very interesting! Remember that there are more important things than how attractive a boy is, or you could end up getting hurt.

Mostly b): You know that a boyfriend is not worth having if he treats you badly. And because you respect yourself, a boy has to respect you, too, before you'll even think about going out with him. This means that you are most likely to fall in love with a kind and sweet boy who will really show that he loves you!

Mostly c): The most important thing for you is that your boyfriend is just right for you, and that you have plenty of interests in common. If a boy can really make you laugh, he has a chance of winning your heart.

ÜBUNG 22:

1. a 2. g 3. e 4. c 5. b 6. d 7. f

ÜBUNG 23:

1. richtig 2. richtig 3. falsch 4. falsch 5. richtig 6. falsch 7. falsch

ÜBUNG 24:

1. better 2. easier 3. more interesting 4. worst 5. further 6. less 7. most confident

ÜBUNG 25:

1. c 2. b 3. c

ÜBUNG 26:

1. stressed 2. better 3. strangely 4. same 5. larger 6. silly 7. open 9. friends

ÜBUNG 27:

1. can't 2. She's, isn't 3. hasn't, she'll 4. doesn't, he's 5. she'd, didn't 6. won't, doesn't

ÜBUNG 28:

1. e 2. c 3. b 4. a 5. d

ÜBUNG 29:

1. at 2. for 3. with, to 4. in front of 5. to, for

ÜBUNG 30:

0–10 points: You don't think of this boy as anything more than a friend. Make sure that he doesn't think that the friendship means more to you than it really does, or you could soon find yourself in a difficult situation.

11–20 points: There is a chance that this could develop into something more, but at the moment there are some problems. If he is just a crush, or if you haven't been together for very long, your feelings could become stronger in the future. But if you have been together for more than a few months, you probably aren't with the right boy. Anyway, give it time, and follow your feelings!

21–30 points: Wow! You have found your perfect match! You love spending time together, and miss him whenever he isn't with you. If he is your crush, you should definitely try and find the courage to ask him out, and if he is already your boyfriend, you are very lucky indeed!

Glossar

to abandon	ablegen
abruptly	abrupt, plötzlich
absorbed	vertieft
act	Darbietung
to act strangely	sich merkwürdig verhalten
to add	hinzufügen
to admit	zugeben
advice	Rat
affectionately	liebevoll
ages ago	vor Ewigkeiten
annoying	lästig, nervig
anxiously	ängstlich
to argue	behaupten, einwenden
to arrange	verabreden, ausmachen
attached	*hier:* angewachsen
attention	Aufmerksamkeit
audience	Publikum
to avoid	vermeiden
ballet routine	Ballettnummer
banner	Transparent, Spruchband
barely	kaum
to be about to do sth.	im Begriff sein, etw. zu tun
beat	Rhythmus, Takt
to beat (beat, beaten) sb.	jmd. schlagen (besiegen)
to be embarrassed	verlegen sein, sich schämen
before long	bald
behaviour	Verhalten
to be mad at sb.	auf jmd. wütend sein
to be pleased	sich freuen
blank	leer
blossom	Blüte
to blush	erröten, rot werden
to bow	sich verbeugen
bowl	Schüssel
brace	Zahnspange
bucket	Eimer

bully	Rüpel
to burst (burst, burst)	(zer)platzen
butterfly	Schmetterling
casual	lässig, locker
to change the subject	das Thema wechseln
changing room	Umkleide
to chat	plaudern
cheek	Wange
to cheer	jubeln
to cheer for sb.	jmd. anfeuern, Beifall klatschen
↯ cheerful	aufgekratzt
chocolate bar	Schokoriegel
chubby	mollig
to clap	klatschen
clarinet	Klarinette
clenched	geballt
clumsy	unbeholfen
to collapse	zusammenbrechen
to collapse onto one's bed	aufs Bett fallen
to collect	abholen
to comfort sb.	jmd. trösten
to comment on	sich äußern zu
complicated	kompliziert
to compliment sth.	über etw. Komplimente machen
confession	Geständnis
confidently	selbstbewusst
confused	verwirrt
constantly	ständig
contest	Wettbewerb
convinced	überzeugt
couple	Paar
courage	Mut
crowd	Menge
cruel	gemein
crumpled	zerknüllt
crush	Schwarm
curious	neugierig
curls	Locken
curtain	Vorhang
to cut the ground from under sb.'s feet	jmd. den Boden unter den Füßen wegziehen

deep scarlet	scharlachrot
deep-fried	frittiert
defensively	verteidigend
definite	sicher, fest
delight	Freude, Entzücken
delighted	sehr erfreut
to demand	verlangen
to deserve	verdienen
desperately	verzweifelt
despite	trotz
determined	entschlossen
distant	distanziert
distracted	abgelenkt
to dread sth.	etw. fürchten
drone	Brummen
drum	Trommel, Schlagzeug
eagerly	eifrig, begierig
edge	Ecke
effort	Anstrengung
either way	so oder so
electric current	elektrischer Strom
embarrassing	peinlich
energetic	schwungvoll
to enter a competition	sich für einen Wettbewerb anmelden
enthusiastic	begeistert
equally	gleichermaßen
eventually	schließlich
excitement	Aufregung
to exclaim	ausrufen
excuse	Ausrede
expectantly	erwartungsvoll
to fall (fell, fallen) for sb.	in jmd. verknallt sein
⚡ to fancy sb.	auf jmd. stehen
to feel comfortable	sich wohlfühlen
to feel homesick	Heimweh haben
to feel transported to	sich versetzt fühlen nach
firmly	nachdrücklich
fist	Faust
to flash through	aufblitzen in
flattering	schmeichelhaft

flawlessly	fehlerlos
to flip	einen Salto schlagen
to flood out	heraussprudeln
to flow	*hier:* wallen
focused on	bezogen auf
full volume	volle Lautstärke
to gasp	nach Luft ringen
ϟ geek	Streber(in)
gently	sanft, behutsam
genuine	echt, aufrichtig
to get sth. exactly right	etw. genau richtig machen
to giggle	kichern
to give sb. a makeover	jmd. stylen
glad	froh
gloomily	bedrückt
to glow	glühen
gorgeous	umwerfend
to grab	(er)greifen
gradually	allmählich, nach und nach
grateful	dankbar
ϟ Guess what!	Stell dir vor!
to guess	vermuten, erraten
hardly ever	fast nie
harshly	barsch
to head towards home	heimwärts steuern
to hide (hid, hidden)	verstecken
hilarious	urkomisch
honest	ehrlich
horrified	entsetzt
hug	Umarmung
hurt	gekränkt
I'd (had) better	ich sollte besser
imaginary	Schein-, Fantasie-,
to imagine sth.	sich etw. vorstellen
imitation	Nachahmung
impatiently	ungeduldig
impressed	beeindruckt
to improve	verbessern
in a row	in Folge
incredible	unglaublich
infatuation	Verliebtheit

ink	Tinte
to insist	beharren
to interrupt	unterbrechen
in unison	einstimmig
irritation	Verärgerung
It's a deal!	Abgemacht!
it's a shame	es ist schade
jealous	eifersüchtig
jelly	Wackelpudding
judge	Juror(in)
to judge	beurteilen
knee-length	knielang
to knock	anklopfen
knot	Knoten
to lean (leant, leant) in	sich neigen zu
to light (lit, lit) up	erhellen, aufleuchten lassen
loads	jede Menge
loads of	eine Menge
mark	Schulnote
to mask	verbergen
to match	passen zu
mention	Erwähnung
to mention	erwähnen
mess	Durcheinander
mischievous	verschmitzt, spitzbübisch
miserable	unglücklich
to move house	umziehen
move	Bewegung
muddy	schmutzig
to mumble	murmeln
mysterious	geheimnisvoll, rätselhaft
natural dancer	geborene(r) Tänzer(in)
nausea	Übelkeit
necklace	Halskette
no matter how	egal wie
to nod	nicken
notice board	Schwarzes Brett
No way!	Nie im Leben!
to nudge	(an)stupsen
obstacle course	Hindernisparcours
obviously	natürlich, offensichtlich

odd-looking	sonderbar aussehend
to offer	anbieten
one by one	der Reihe nach
only child	Einzelkind
out of place	fehl am Platz
to overcome (overcame, overcome)	überwinden
to overhear (overheard, overheard)	belauschen
to owe	schulden
painful	schmerzhaft
pathetic	erbärmlich
patient	geduldig
PE (physical education)	Sport(unterricht)
to perch on sth.	auf etw. sitzen
performance	Auftritt
performer	Darsteller(in)
to persuade	überreden
to picture sth.	sich etw. vorstellen
pile	Haufen
pillow	Kopfkissen
pitch	Feld
playfully	scherzhaft
to pound	heftig schlagen
to pour	schütten
to prefer	lieber mögen, vorziehen
to pretend	so tun, als ob
prize	Gewinn
progress	Fortschritt
to promise	versprechen
properly	richtig
to pulse	pulsieren
to punch	schlagen (mit der Faust)
puzzled	ratlos, verblüfft
to reappear	wieder auftauchen
reassurance	Bestätigung
to reassure	versichern
reassuringly	beruhigend
to recognize	wiedererkennen
to regret sth.	etw. bedauern
relieved	erleichtert

to remind	erinnern
to rip sth. open	etw. aufreißen
rude	unhöflich
runner's up prize	zweiter Preis
to rush	eilen, rennen
to scold	(aus)schimpfen
to score a goal	ein Tor schießen
selfish	egoistisch
shade	Farbton, Abtönung
to shake (shook, shaken) loose	abschütteln
to shimmer	schimmern
to shrug	die Schultern zucken
to shuffle	schlurfen
sigh	Seufzer
to sign up	sich anmelden
sing-song	melodisch
skinny	dünn
to skip a beat	einen Schlag aussetzen (Herz)
sleepover	Übernachtung (bei Freunden)
slightest hint	geringste Andeutung
slightly	leicht, ein bisschen
snoring	schnarchend
speechless	sprachlos
to spot	erblicken
to stand out from	sich abheben von
to stare	anstarren
to stay in touch	in Kontakt bleiben
to stay still	still halten
straight away	auf Anhieb, sofort
streak	Strahl
strings	Saiten
to struggle	kämpfen, sich abmühen
to stutter	stammeln, stottern
subject	*hier:* Unterrichtsfach
subtle	dezent
suggestion	Vorschlag
to suit sb.	jmd. stehen
sunset	Sonnenuntergang
to support sb.	jmd. unterstützen
to suppose	annehmen, denken
surrounded by	umgeben von

to suspect	vermuten
suspiciously	argwöhnisch
to sweat	schwitzen
to take (took, taken) over	die Führung übernehmen
to tease	necken, ärgern
to tell (told, told) sb. off	jdn. ausschimpfen
to tend to	neigen zu
term	Trimester
text (message)	SMS
though	aber, doch
throat	Hals, Kehle
to tidy one's hair	seine Haare richten/ordnen
tied up	zusammengebunden
to tighten	enger werden
to tingle	prickeln
to tremble	zittern
to trickle down	herunterlaufen
to trip	stolpern
trophy	Pokal
uncontrollably	unkontrollierbar
unexpected	unerwartet
unfortunately	leider
unhealthy	ungesund
unpleasant	unangenehm
to upset (upset, upset)	beunruhigen
to vote	abstimmen, bewerten
waist	Taille
water gun	Wasserpistole
to wave	winken
weird	eigenartig, schräg
wheelchair	Rollstuhl
whereas	wohingegen
wide awake	hellwach
to wince	zusammenzucken
wise	klug, weise
worry	Sorge